Jonathan Lax

7/22/?

Dear Lex,

Happy
Sight singing.

Cheers,

[signature]

Sight - Singing
and
Related Skills

AnneMarie de Zeeuw

State University of New York at Stony Brook

Roger E. Foltz

Temple University

University Stores, Incorporated

P. O. Box 7756 • Austin, Texas 78712

To Janet McGaughey

a devoted teacher and remarkable
person to whom this book, we
ourselves, and many students
are deeply indebted.

Preface

It has been observed by the authors of this text that the sight-singing manuals currently available fit into two categories accommodating differing philosophies of the college sight-singing class. One view is that a sight-singing class should be regarded as a music reading class, with the voice to be used as one of the many instruments that might be available to the members of the class. On the other hand, the sight-singing class has been conceived by some as a situation where students develop not only music reading but related aural skills principally through the voice. It is the latter of these two philosophies that best describes the views of the authors and of this text.

A necessary tool for every musician is the ability to produce vocally a given line of music, often at sight. This has been proven beneficial not only as an analytical tool but also as an important and convenient means of musical communication, especially for the instructor in the classroom and for the choral or instrumental conductor. Sight-singing is also viewed by the authors as a complementary aid in the development of listening skills. The two processes may be very readily fused; for instance, an exercise may be used first for some kind of dictation or critical listening practice before it is sung. Using these skills in combination helps to cultivate the habit of attentiveness and the exercise of critical judgment in class.

In the area of aural skills, one technique of sight-singing practice comes to the forefront. An important goal of an ear training class is to develop the skill of aural perception of a piece of music without having to produce it vocally. For the development of this skill the authors recommend frequent practice of the following materials in a manner that has been named "silent sight-singing." In this technique, the student begins to sing an exercise as usual; upon a given cue, he stops producing sound but continues to "sing" the exercise mentally. Upon a second cue, he resumes the exercise vocally. This practice should be continued until the student is fluent in changing from "silent" to audible sight-singing.

It is necessary that the student as well as the instructor be aware of proper vocal techniques at all times. It is quite obvious that all are not possessors of fine vocal instruments, but the fundamentals of good vocal technique should be kept in mind. Many times, intonation problems are caused by improper vocal production; for this reason, some helpful basic vocal suggestions are presented in the appendix of this book.

Preface.

Sight-Singing and Related Skills is divided into five chapters: 1) Rhythm 2) Interval Classes and Pitch Sets 3) Clef Studies and Transposition 4) Examples from Literature 5) Supplementary Materials. For the most part, no attempt has been made to place the exercises in any sort of graded arrangement. The criteria for grading sight-singing materials are so numerous and varied that it is felt that any such attempt would only add to the existing confusion. Instead, the authors have tried to organize the materials in a clear manner that will facilitate the selection of examples from the various chapters to correlate with the instructor's particular theory program. An individual assignment will ordinarily consist of selected exercises from several chapters.

It should be noted that students using this book are assumed to have certain basic music reading skills. In consequence, the level of preparation of the class will determine when in the curriculum the use of this text is begun.

The authors have attempted to present a wide variety of concepts in sight-singing. Some of the more traditional ideas have received a little less attention than is perhaps usual, not due to any value judgment but rather to the fact that there is such a vast number of books which quite adequately express these concepts. It is believed that enough diverse exercises and materials have been brought together so that this book can be integrated into any theory program. Although much stress has been placed on actual singing in this book, the authors do wish to point out the importance of the related skills that need to be incorporated into sight-singing. The accomplished sight-singer is always aware of tonal orientation, intervallic relationships, rhythmic structure, and formal outlay, and able to deal with such matters as transposition and reading C clefs; he has the capacity to imagine the sound of what he sees in the printed score.

In the course of the preparation of this book, the authors have received the help and encouragement of many people. We acknowledge gratefully: Janet McGaughey and Kent Kennan for their numerous suggestions and many hours of proofreading; Rebecca Baltzer for her invaluable advice and assistance in the preparation of many of the selections from the Middle Ages and Renaissance; Karl Korte for providing compositions for Chapter V; Jerry Dean and Eldon Black for their articles on chromatic solfège and singing respectively; James Cook and Charles Turner who provided transcriptions for Chapter IV; and Patricia Andrews, William Cory, Charles Ward, and Kelly Ward, who assisted us greatly in a variety of ways. We thank also Sterling Swift of University Stores, Inc., and we thank the following publishers for permission to reprint copyright materials: C.F. Peters Corporation; International Music Company; G. Schirmer, Inc.; Belwin-Mills Publishing Corp.; Boosey and Hawkes, Inc.; Carl Fischer, Inc.; Summy-Birchard Company; and Theodore Presser Company. Finally, we would like to acknowledge the many students who have assisted in the formation of some of the concepts expressed in this book.

August 1973

Anne Marie de Zeeuw
and
Roger E. Foltz

Contents

viii

Contents.

I *Rhythm*

Suggested modes of performance:

One-part examples:
1. Intone the rhythm on a neutral syllable such as <u>ta</u> and tap or clap the beat. Intoning the rhythm affords precise control of the duration of sounds. Tapping or clapping the beat permits the beat to be sensed physically; this facilitates the performance of syncopated rhythms in particular.
2. Intone the rhythm using rhythmic recitation syllables of the type developed by McHose and Tibbs;[1] tap or clap the beat.
3. Intone the rhythm while conducting. Conducting enhances mental and physical awareness of the meter as well as the beat, and, unlike tapping, it is silent. It presents a co-ordination problem at first for many students, however.
4. Tap or clap the rhythm while counting beats. (Tapping also permits the execution of two or more lines by a single performer.)
5. Tap the rhythm with one hand and the beat with the other.
6. Tap the rhythm with one hand and conduct with the other.
7. Intone, tap, or clap the rhythm without the auxiliary techniques of tapping or counting the beat or conducting. These techniques are helpful in learning rhythms, but they are annoying mannerisms when they carry over into performance, and dependence on them must be avoided.

Two-part examples:
1. Combine intoning, tapping, clapping, counting, and/or conducting in any way feasible for a single performer.
2. Perform as ensemble drills.

---

[1] Allen Irvine McHose and Ruth Northup Tibbs, <u>Sight-Singing Manual</u> (3rd ed.; New York: Appleton-Century-Crofts, Inc., 1957).

Rhythm.

Practice suggestions:

1. Locate the beats; mark them mentally. In some cases the instructor may wish to permit students to mark beats in pencil; it is often helpful to do so in examples where visual cues such as beams are lacking or where beats fall on rests. In exercises involving meters with asymmetrical beats, it is also frequently desirable to mark the beats; a system of marking such as the following (which is an adaptation of one first used extensively in Messiaen's works and now employed by many conductors) shows not only the location of beats but also their relative length:

2. Divide the beats. Begin at a slow tempo and build rhythms additively from the divided beats, then increase the tempo.

3. Simplify exercises that present problems. Reduce them to forms in which they may be easily mastered, then reintroduce the original problems one at a time, as in the following example:

4. Do at a rapid tempo some exercises in which the note-value
    of the beat is a half note or greater, and at a slow tempo
    some exercises in which it is an eighth note or smaller.
    Ideally, each example should be done at several different
    tempi.
5. Work with a metronome for accuracy.

****

Exercises involving the beat, multiples of the beat, and divisions of the
beat (one half of a simple beat or one third of a compound beat).

4

Rhythm.

6.

7.

8.

9.

10.

11.

Division of the beat. Simple duple meters.

Rhythm.

Division of the beat. Simple quadruple meters.

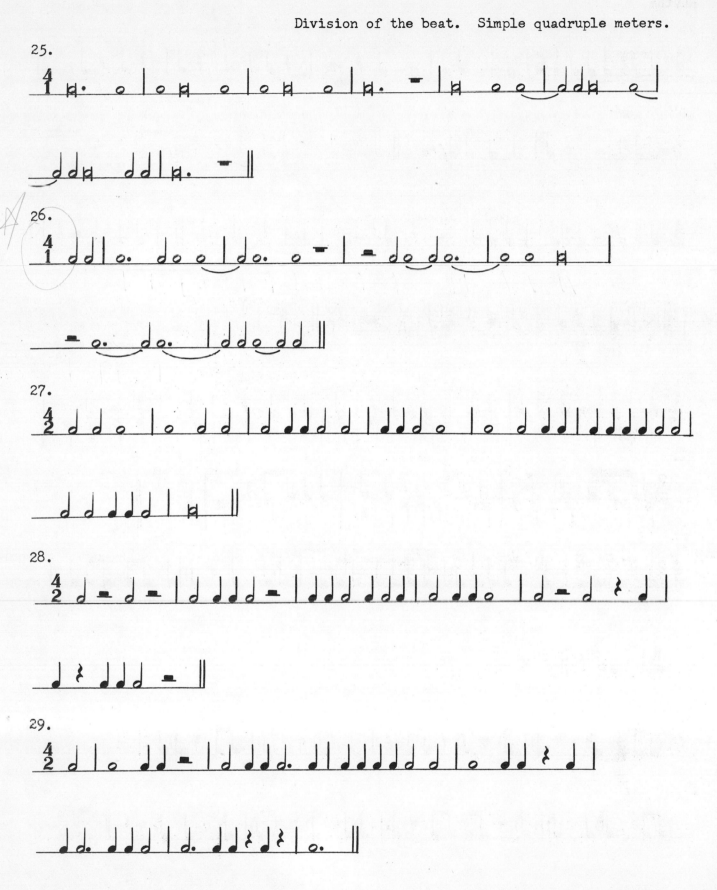

8

Rhythm.

30.

31.

32.

33.

34.

10

Rhythm.

Division of the beat. Simple quadruple and triple meters.

Rhythm.

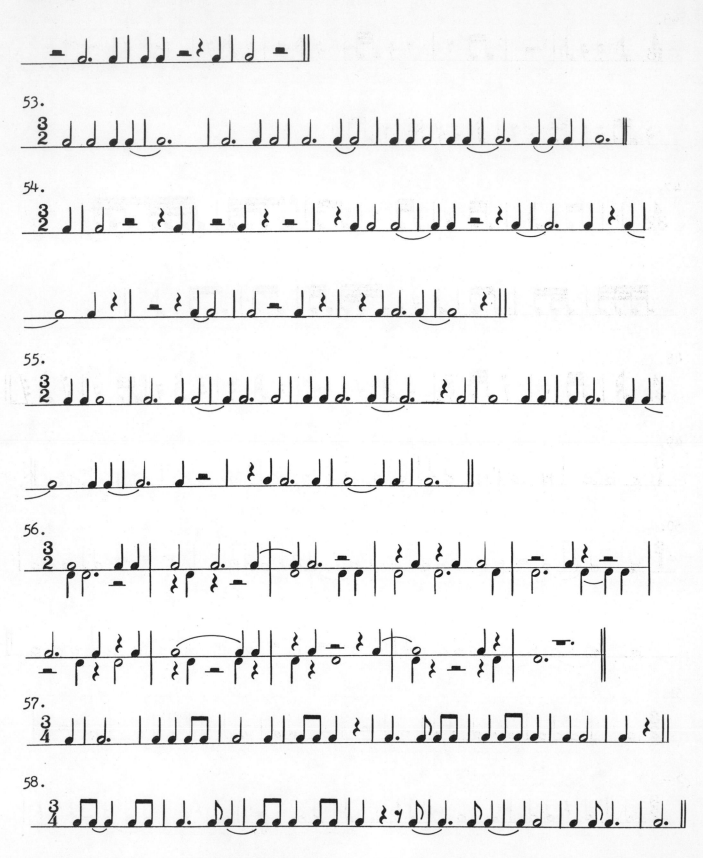

14

Rhythm.

15

Division of the beat. Compound duple meters.

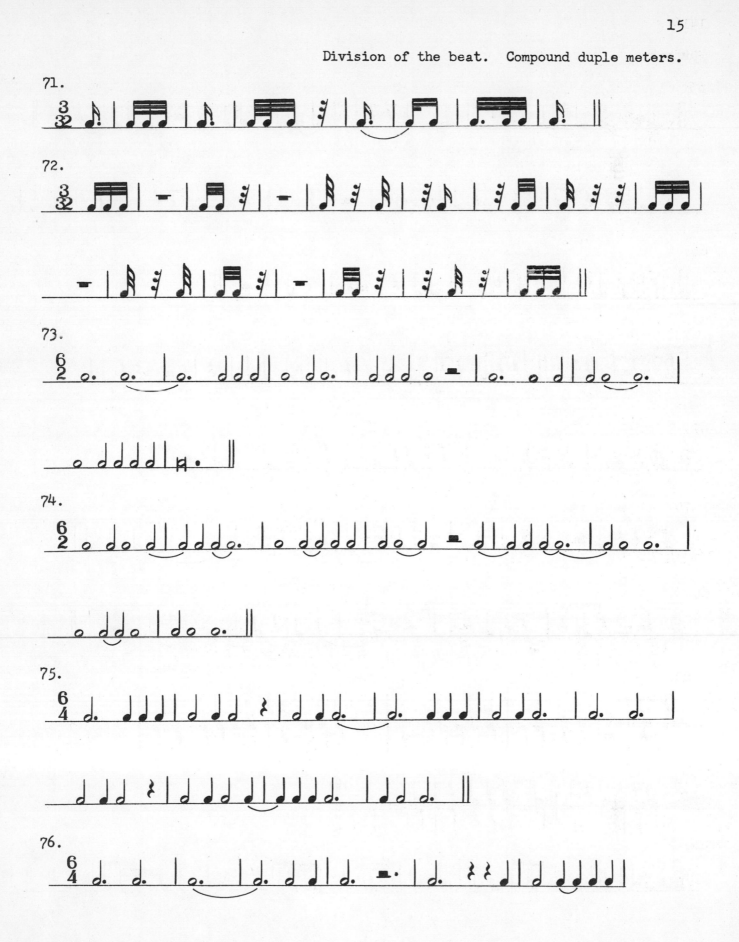

16

Rhythm.

Division of the beat.   Compound duple meters.

18

Rhythm.

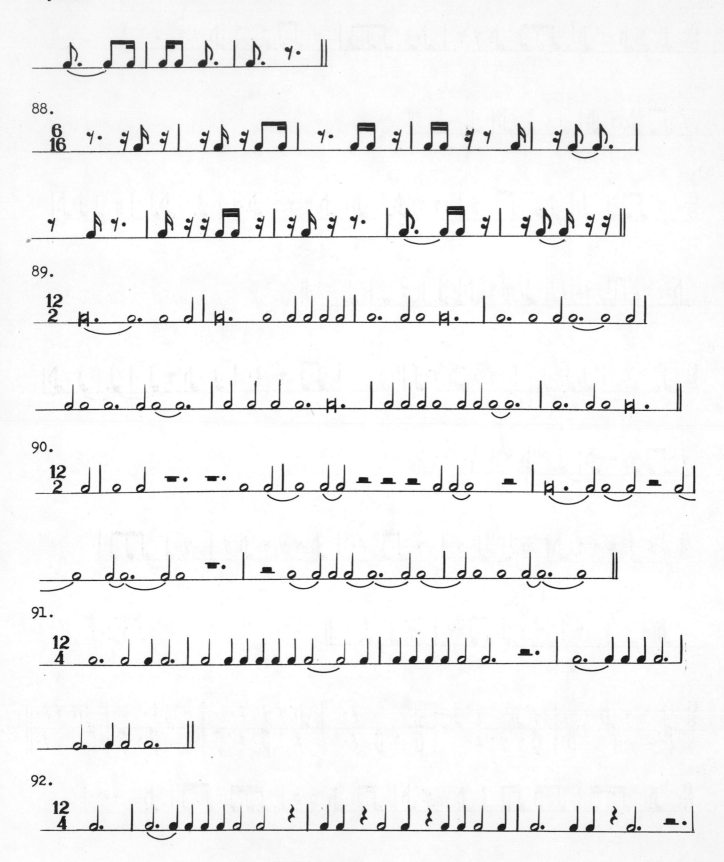

Division of the beat.   Compound quadruple meters.

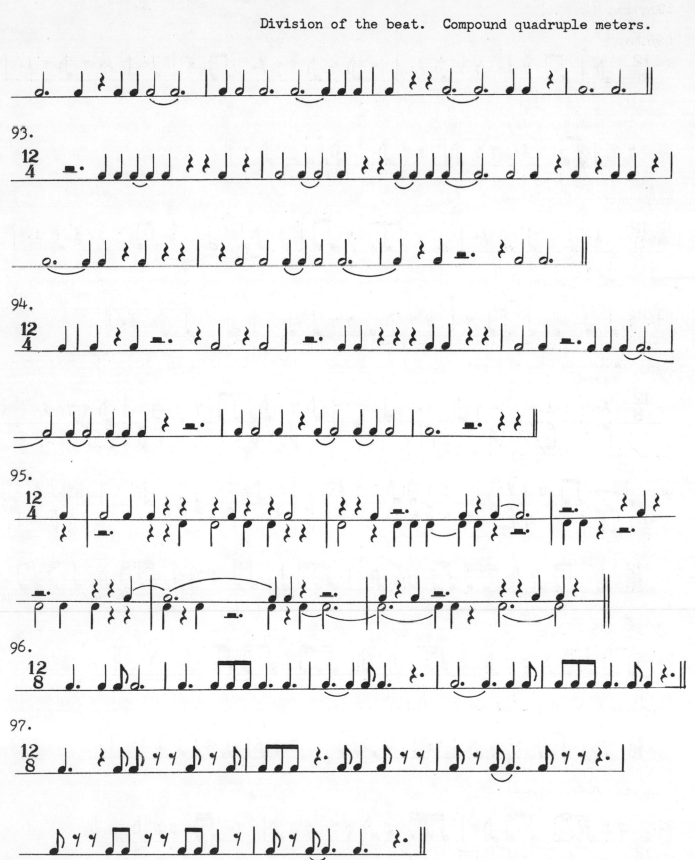

Rhythm.

98.

99.

100.

101.

102.

21

Division of the beat. Compound triple meters.

22

Rhythm

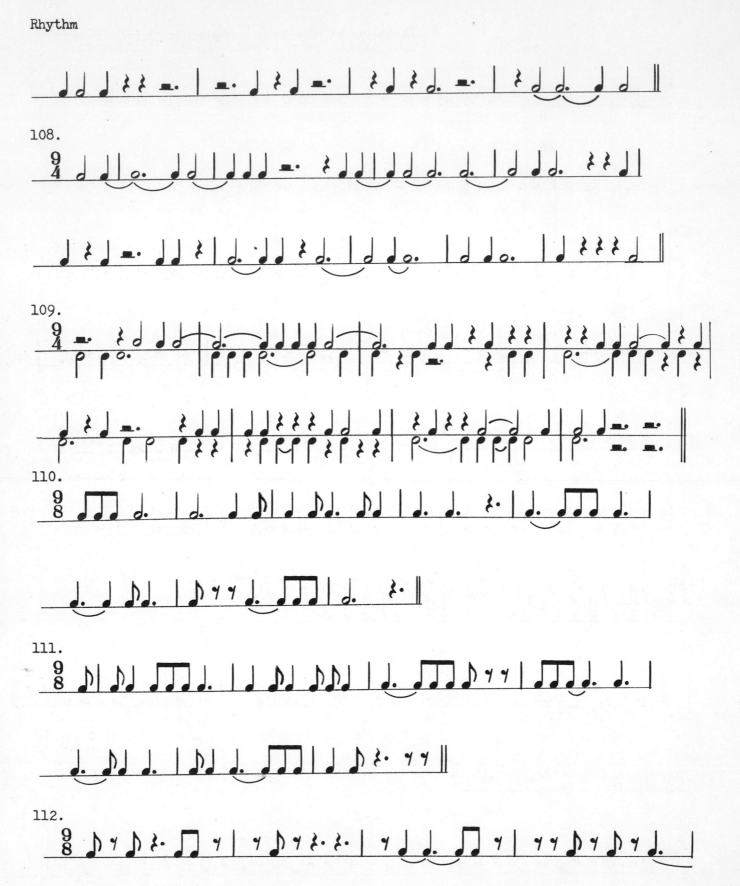

Division of the beat. Compound triple meters.
Subdivision of the beat. Simple duple meters.

Exercises involving subdivision of the beat (one fourth of a simple beat or one sixth of a compound beat).

24

Rhythm.

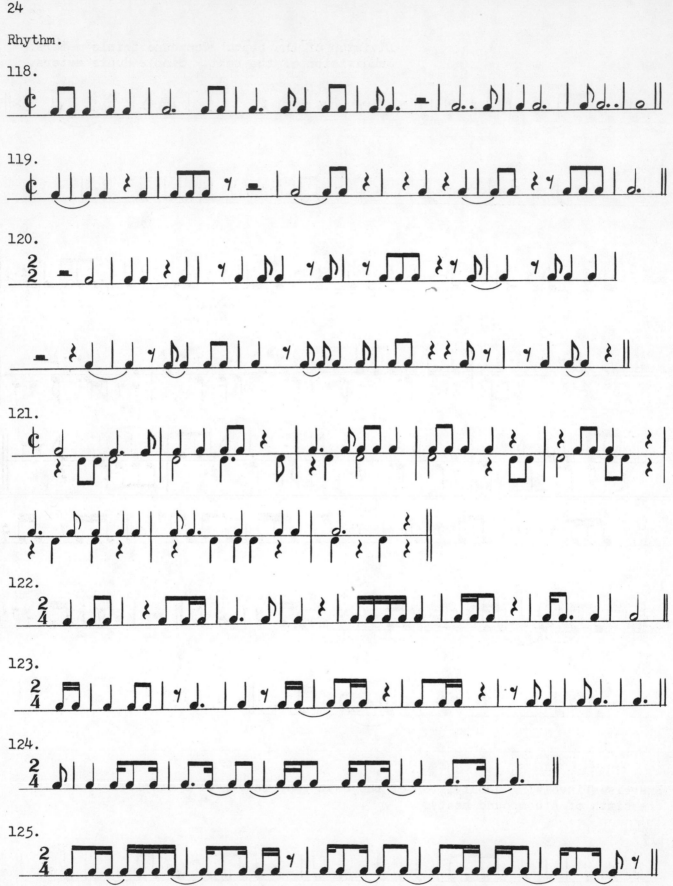

126.

26

Rhythm.

133.

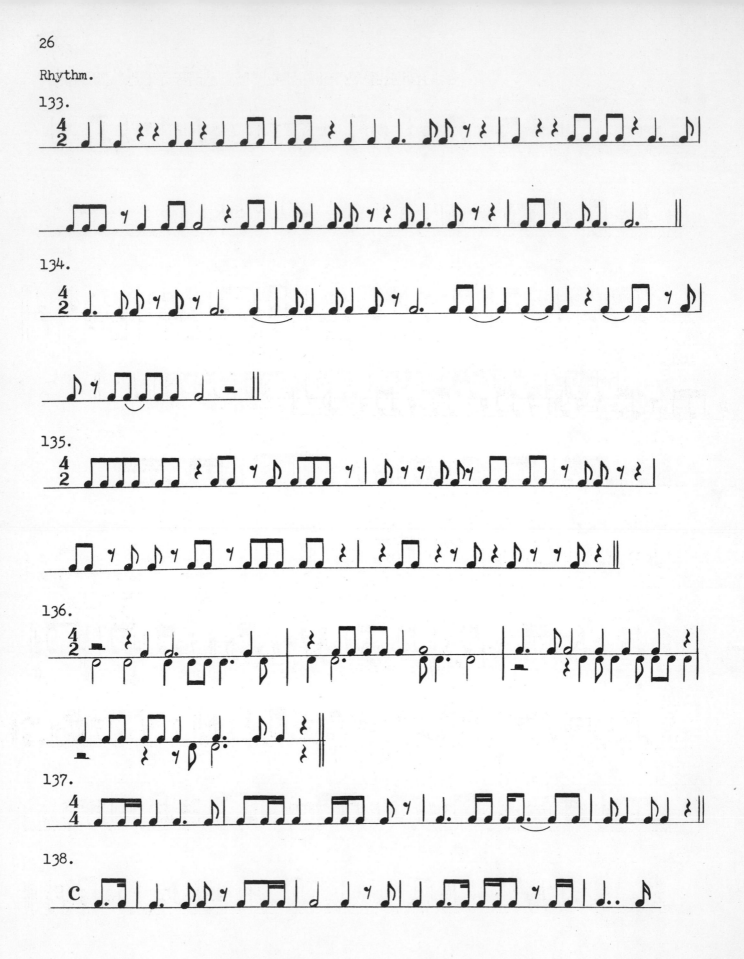

134.

135.

136.

137.

138.

Rhythm.

144.

145.

146.

147.

148.

149.

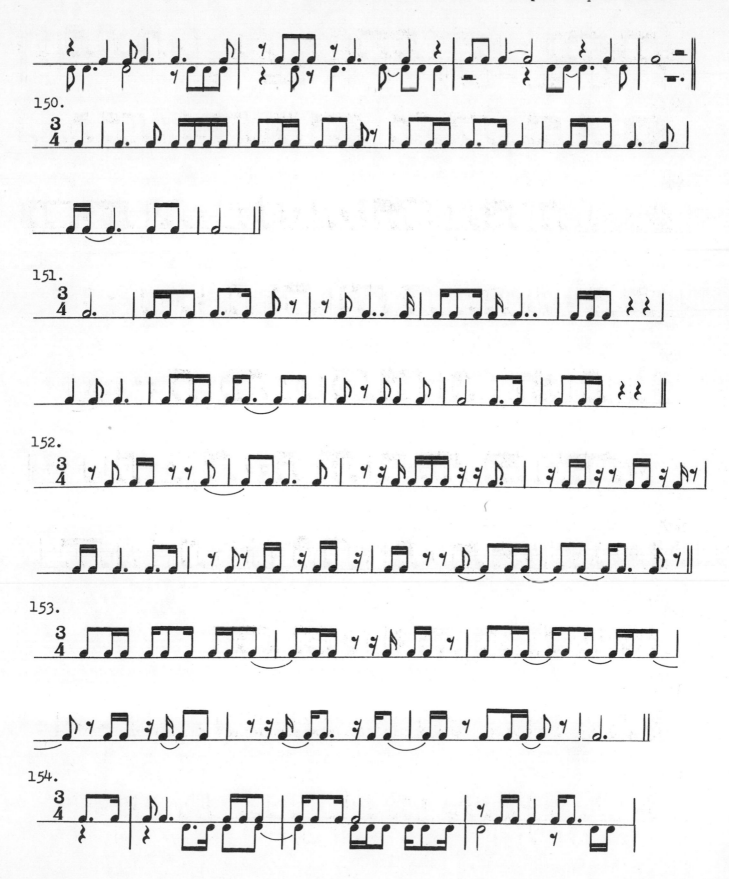

150.

151.

152.

153.

154.

30

Rhythm.

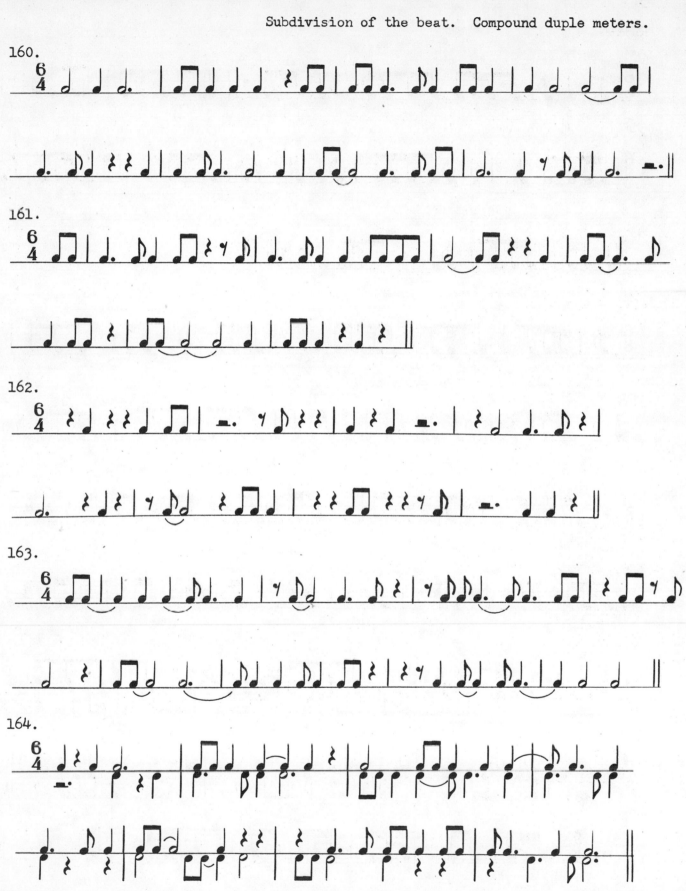

32

Rhythm.

165.

166.

167.

168.

169.

170.

Subdivision of the beat. Compound duple and quadruple meters.

34

Rhythm.

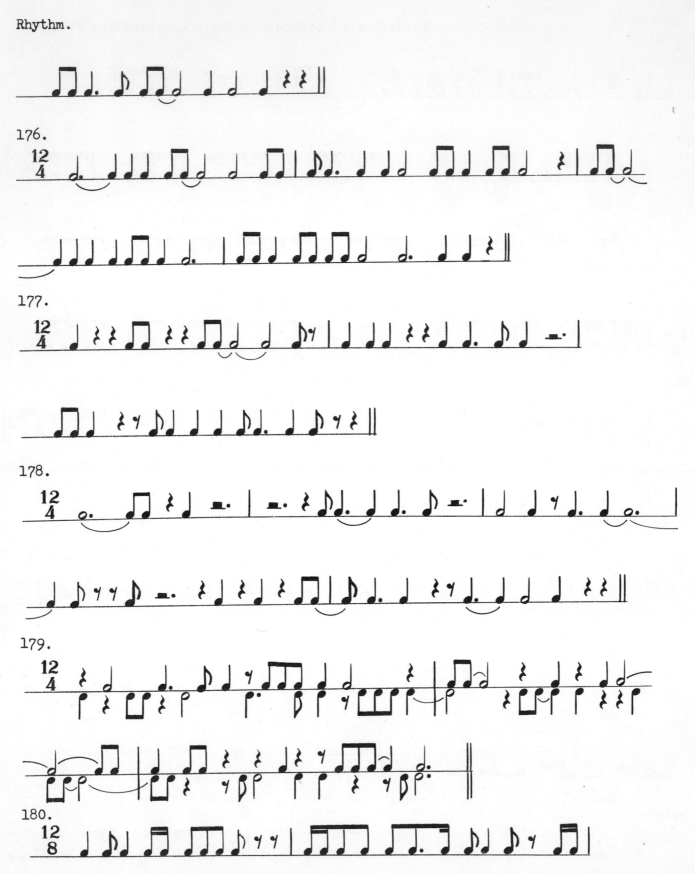

176.

177.

178.

179.

180.

Subdivision of the beat.   Compound quadruple meters.

36

Rhythm.

186.

187.

188.

189.

190.

191.

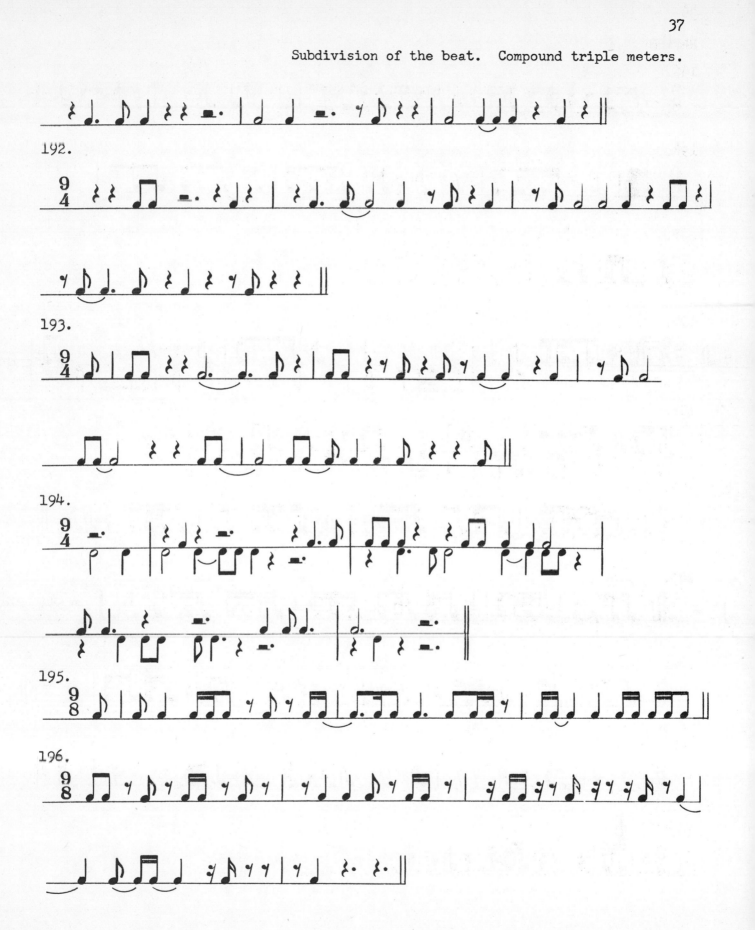

38

Rhythm.

39

Triplets.

Exercises involving triplets, duplets, and other groupings.

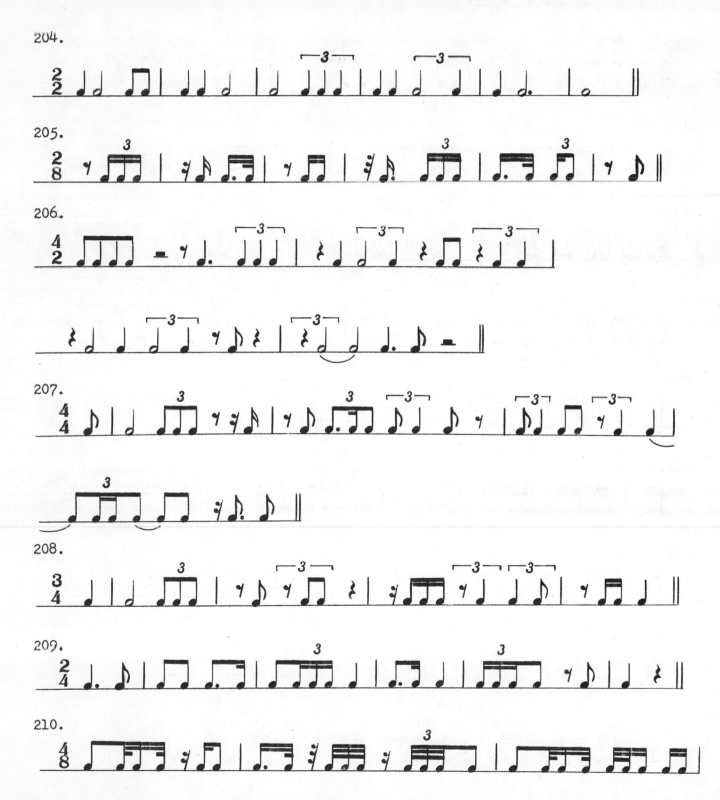

Rhythm.

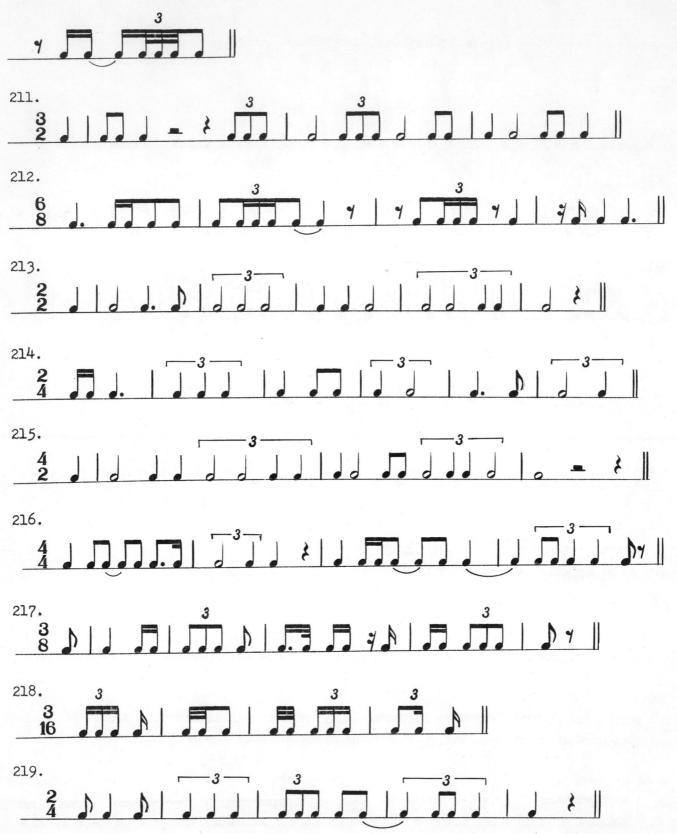

Triplets and duplets.

42

Rhythm.

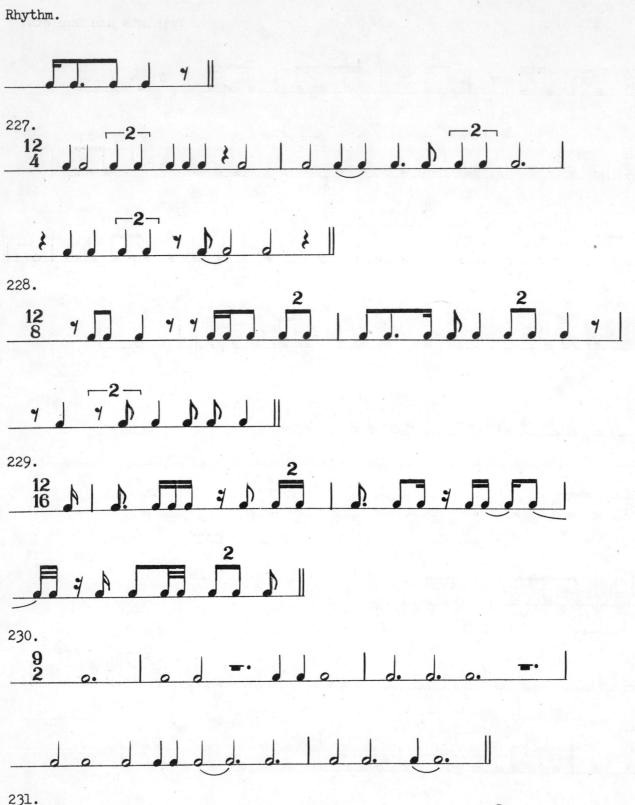

43

Duplets and other groupings.

44

Rhythm.

Exercises involving asymmetrical meters, changing meters, polyrhythm, and polymeter.

244.

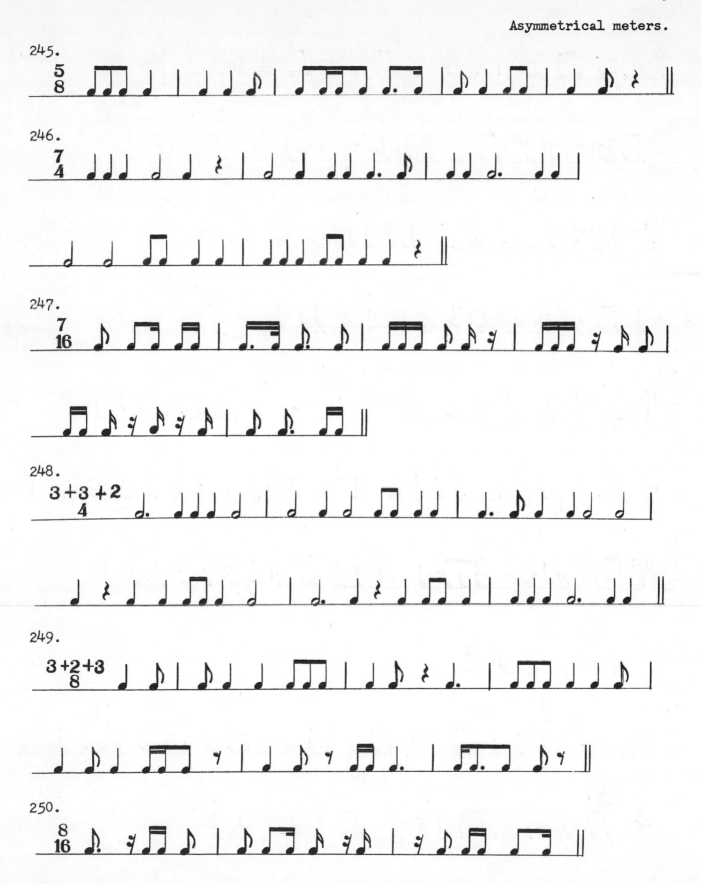

Rhythm.

251.

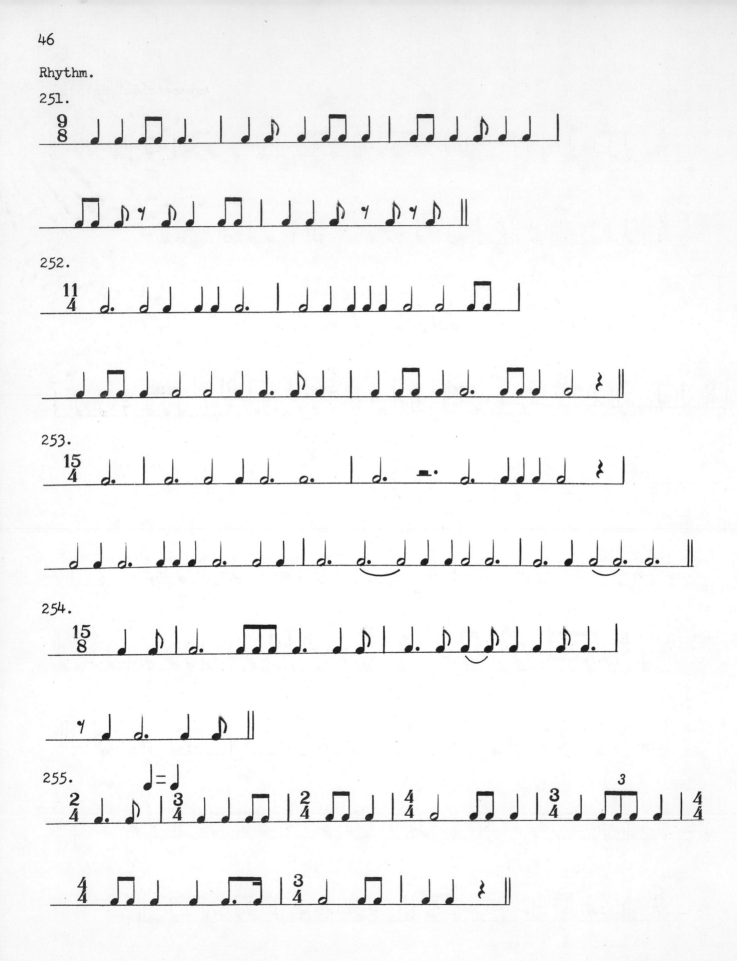

Changing meters.

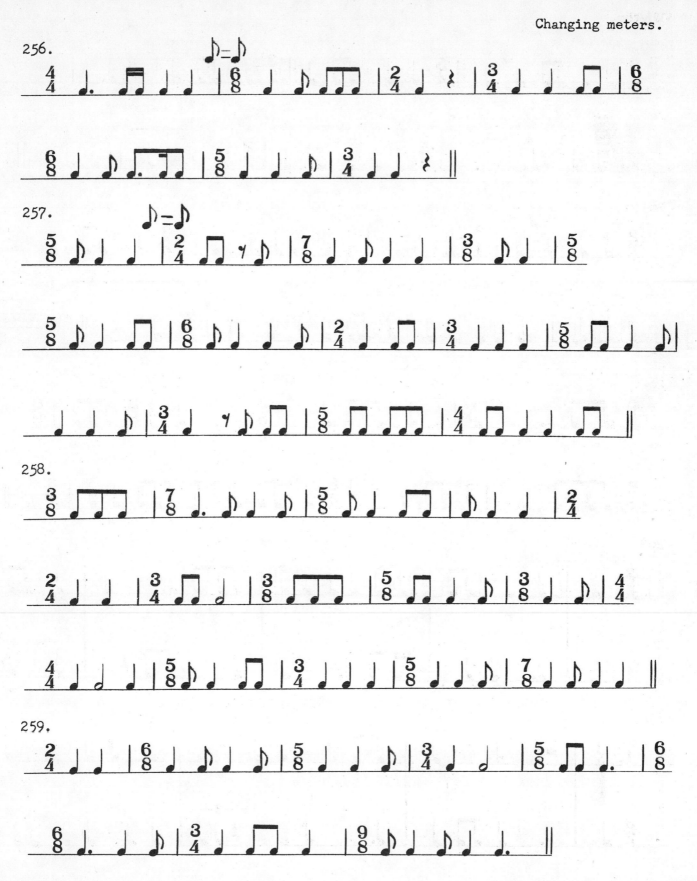

Rhythm.

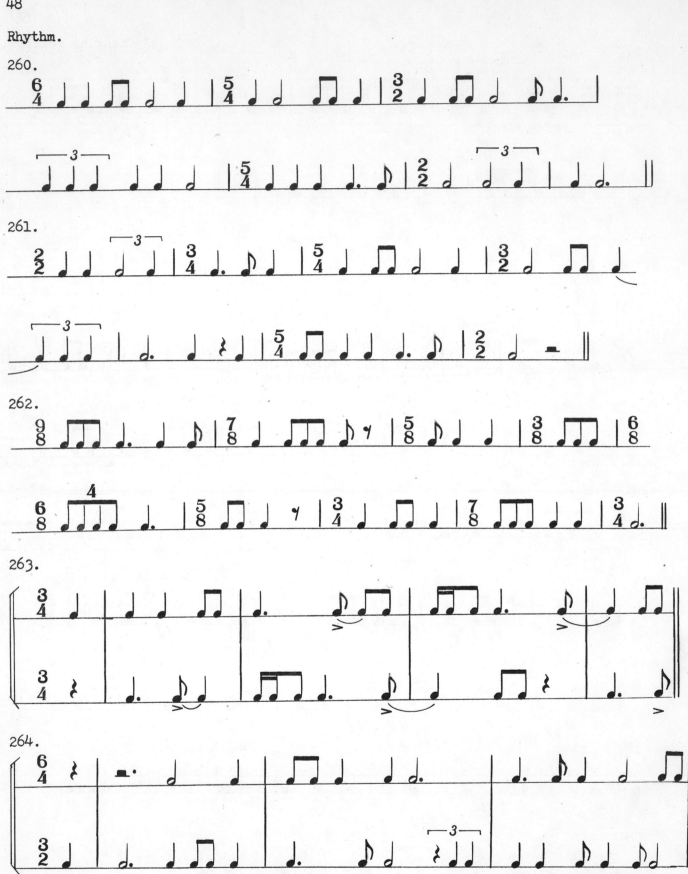

Polymeter.

265.

II Interval Classes and Pitch Sets

INTERVAL CLASSES

Explanatory note: An interval, its complement (inversion), their compound forms, and their enharmonic equivalents together comprise an <u>interval class</u>. Interval classes are numbered in accordance with the number of semitones contained in the smallest representative of each class. For example, IC I (interval class I) consists of minor seconds (augmented primes), major sevenths (diminished octaves), minor ninths, and so on.

Suggested modes of performance:
   1. Sing texted examples with either of the texts provided.
   2. Sing with solfège.
   3. Sing with letter names of pitches.
   4. Sing on a neutral syllable.

Practice suggestions:
   1. Begin the introductory exercise for each interval class on several different pitches, using letter names, fixed-do solfège, or some other means of naming the pitches sung.
   2. Sing all other exercises at the indicated pitch. Octave equivalents of pitches that lie in an awkward vocal range may be used.

****

50

Exercises involving interval class I.

52

Interval classes and pitch sets.

277.

278.

Interval class II.

279.

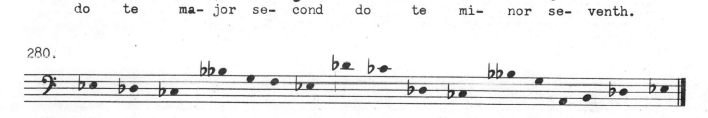

Do te ma- jor se- cond   do te mi- nor se- venth

La la   la la

do te ma- jor se- cond do te mi- nor se- venth.

280.

281.

Interval classes and pitch sets.

282.

56

Interval classes and pitch sets.

Interval class III.

292.

{Me do mi-nor third {me do ma- jor sixth
{La la {la la

me do mi-nor third me do ma- jor sixth.

293.

294.

295.

296.

Grazioso

297.

Giocoso

Interval classes and pitch sets.

Interval class IV.

302.

{Mi do ma-jor third {mi do mi-nor sixth
{La la {La la

mi do ma-jor third mi do mi-nor sixth.

303.

304.

305.

306.

Tranquillo

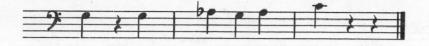

307.

308.

Andante

309.

Animato

60

Interval classes and pitch sets.

310.

311.

Vivace

Interval class V.

312.

Fa do per- fect fourth   fa do per- fect fifth
La la   la la

fa do per- fect fourth   fa do per- fect fifth.

313.

314.

315.

316.

Not too fast

317.

Grave

62

Interval classes and pitch sets.

318.

319. Briskly

320.

321.

Interval class VI.

322.

Interval classes and pitch sets.

329.

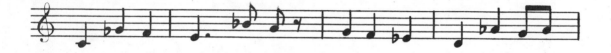

330.

Lively

Interval classes and pitch sets.

331.

PITCH SETS

Explanatory note: For the purposes of this text, the term <u>pitch</u> <u>set</u> will
be used to signify any designated group of pitch classes. The term thus
subsumes sets as diverse as a major scale or an arbitrary three-pitch set.
The present chapter does not involve the type of material wherein the set
is treated in serial fashion.

Suggested modes of performance: See INTERVAL CLASSES, p. 50.

Practice suggestions:
1. Where it is not given, determine the pitch set used in each
   example and sing the set before doing the example.
2. Work on pitch and rhythm separately if necessary: intone
   or tap the rhythm of an exercise, then sing the pitches in
   equal durations, and finally sing the example as it is
   written.
3. Use a metronome to check the tempi of examples for which
   metronome markings are given. If no metronome is available,
   a watch or clock may be used. A watch ticks five times per
   second, a clock four times; thus, for example, at M.M. 120
   the beat lasts two ticks of a clock or two and a half ticks
   of a watch.

****

Three-pitch sets.

338. Stravinsky: Histoire du Soldat

339. Ravel: Quartet in F Major

68

Interval classes and pitch sets.

340. Bartók: String Quartet No. 1

Four-pitch sets.

341.

342.

343.

344.

345.

346.

347. Gregorian chant: Requiem Mass, Introit

Te de- cet hy- mnus De- us in Si- on, et ti- bi

red- de- tur vo- tum in Je- ru- sa- lem:

348. Brumel: Missa super Dringhs

A- gnus De-   i,

qui tol-lis pec- ca-   ta   mun-   di,

349. Fauré: Requiem, Op. 48

do- na   e- is   do- mi- ne   dona e-is   re- quiem

350. Debussy: Danse

Allegretto

351. Ives: Concord Sonata

Interval classes and pitch sets.

Five-pitch sets.

359. Gregorian chant: Mass of the Christmas vigil, Communion

Re- ve- la- bi- tur glo- ri- a

Do- mi- ni:

360. Mussorgsky: Pictures at an Exhibition, Promenade

Moderato comodo assai e con delicatezza.

361. Glazunov: Symphony No. 3, Op. 33

dolce

cresc. poco

362. Debussy: Nuages

Un peu animé

très expressif

72

Interval classes and pitch sets.

363. Prokofieff: Quartet No. 2, Op. 92

364. Prokofieff: Quartet No. 2, Op. 92

Whole-tone scale

365.

ma-jor se-cond.   simile

366. Debussy: L'Isle joyeuse

367. Debussy: La Mer

Animé et tumultueux (♩ = 96)

368. Bartók: String Quartet No. 1

♩ = 150   dolciss.

Interval classes and pitch sets.

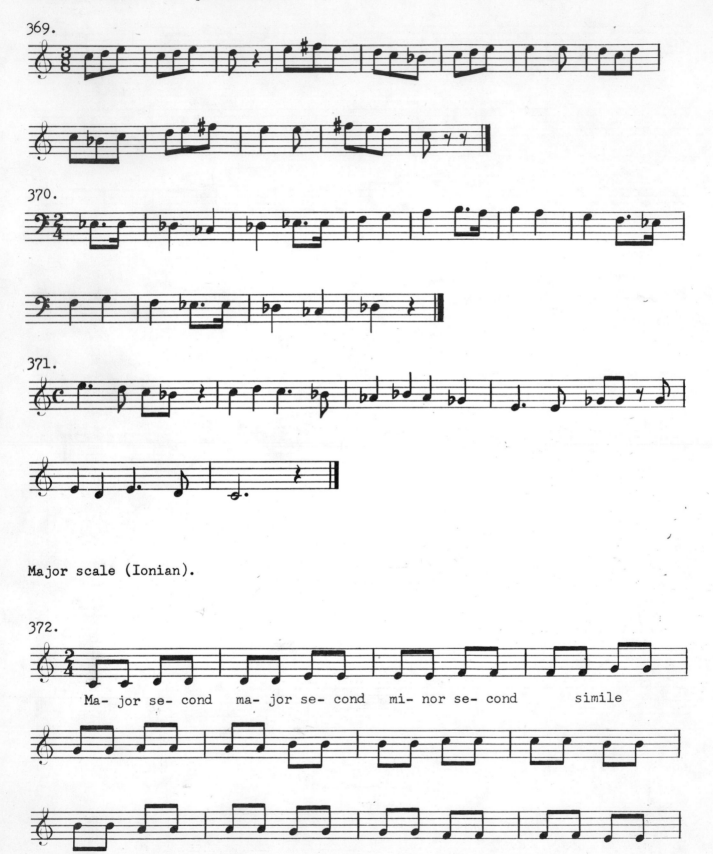

Major scale (Ionian).

373.

374.

375.

376.

377.

Interval classes and pitch sets.

378.

379.

380.

381.

382.

Major scale. Natural minor scale.

383.

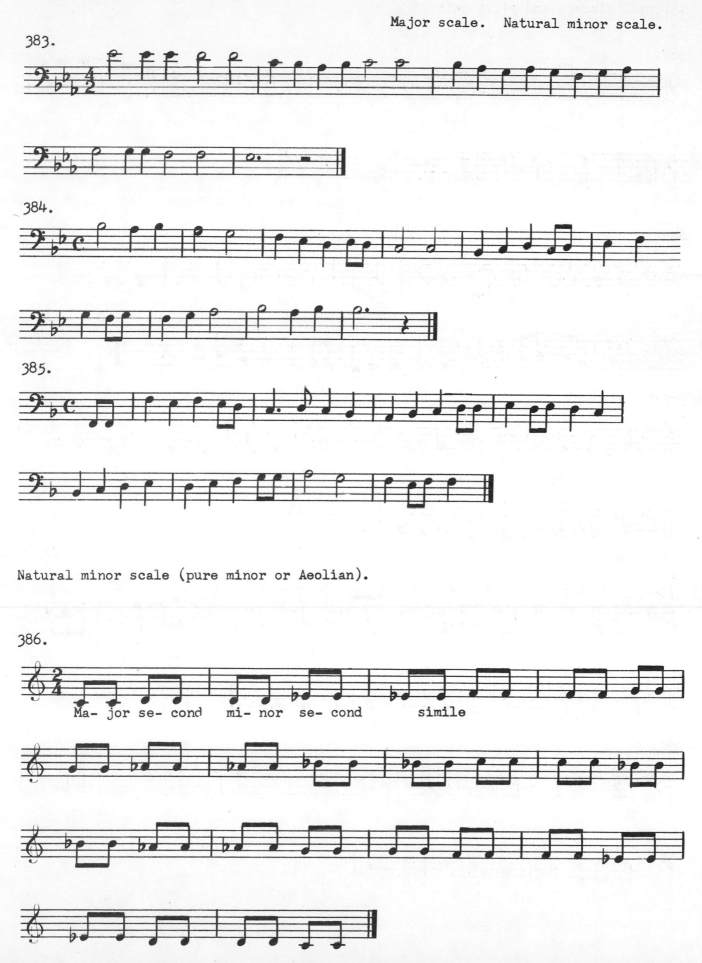

384.

385.

Natural minor scale (pure minor or Aeolian).

386.

Ma- jor se- cond   mi- nor se- cond   simile

78

Interval classes and pitch sets.

Natural minor scale.

392.

393.

394.

395.

396.

Interval classes and pitch sets.

397.

398.

399.

Harmonic minor scale.

400.

Ma-jor se- cond mi- nor se- cond   simile

Harmonic minor scale.

401.

402.

403.

Interval classes and pitch sets.

404.

407.

408. Gregorian chant: Mass of the fourth Saturday in Advent, Introit

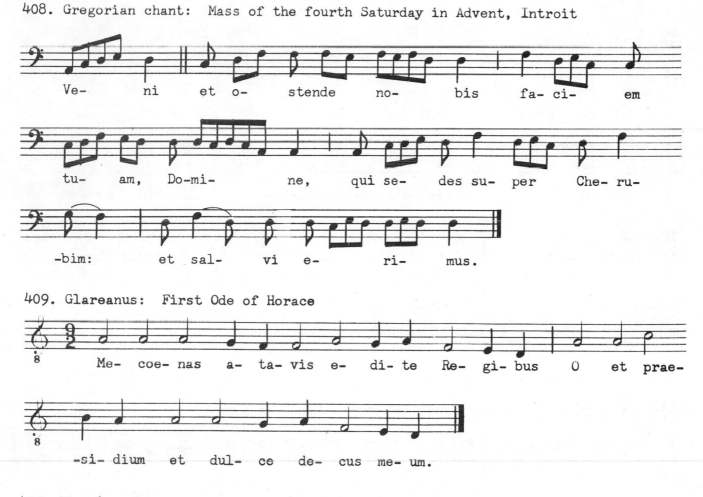

Ve- ni et o- stende no- bis fa- ci- em

tu- am, Do-mi- ne, qui se- des su- per Che- ru-

-bim: et sal- vi e- ri- mus.

409. Glareanus: First Ode of Horace

Me- coe- nas a- ta- vis e- di- te Re- gi- bus O et prae-

-si- dium et dul- ce de- cus me- um.

410. Bartók: Fourteen Bagatelles, Op. 6, V

♩=84

p poco marc.

Interval classes and pitch sets.

Phrygian mode.

411.

412. Gregorian chant: Hymn

Pan- ge lin- gua glo-ri- o- si Cor- po- ris my- ste-

-ri- um, San- gui-nis-que pre-ti- o- si, Quem in mun- di

pre- ti- um Fru- ctus ven- tris ge- ne- ro- si Rex

ef- fu- dit gen- ti- um.

413. Bach: Es woll' uns Gott genädig sein

414. Ravel: Quartet in F Major

♩=120

pp très expr.

Lydian mode.

415.

416. Gregorian chant: Votive Mass of the Passion, Offertory

In- sur-re- xe- runt in me vi-

-ri in- i- qui:

417. Debussy: L'Isle joyeuse

Un peu cédé. Molto rubato

p ondoyant et expressif

più *p*

418. Benjamin Britten: War Requiem

pp cresc.

let us____ sleep now,___ let us_____ sleep now,___

dim.

_ let us____ sleep, sleep_____ now,

Interval classes and pitch sets.

Mixolydian mode.

419.

420. Gregorian chant: Mass of Corpus Christi, Communion

Quo- ti- es- cum- que man- du- ca- bi- tis pa- nem hunc, et

ca- li- cem bi- be- tis, mor- tem Do- mi- ni an- nun- ti- a- bi-

-tis, do- nec ve- ni- at: i- ta- que qui- cum-

-que man- du- ca- ve- rit pa- nem, vel bi- be- rit ca- li- cem Do-

-mi- ni in- di- gne, re- us e- rit cor- po- ris et

san- gui- nis Do- mi- ni, Al- le- lu- ia.

421. Plainsong (Bari Sequentiary): Prose on the Holy Crown

Li- be- ra- lis ma- nus De- i Su- e do- mus

spe- ci- e- i Et co- ro- ne tri- um- pho- rum

col- lo- cat in Fran- ci- a.

422. Anonymous (c. 1550):   Geistliche Ringeltenze

Chromatic scale.

423.

424.

425.

Interval classes and pitch sets.

426.

427.

III Clef Studies and Transposition

CLEF STUDIES

Explanatory note: Several studies in the C clefs appear on a staff with the
C line missing. This pedagogical device, which has been employed for a
number of years in classes at the University of Texas at Austin, demonstrates
the relationship of the C clefs to the great staff:

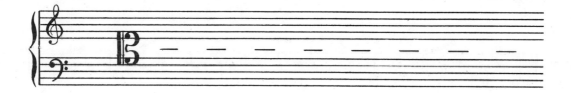

Suggested modes of performance:
    1. Sing with letter names of pitches.
    2. Sing with fixed-do solfège.

✦✦✦✦✦✦✦✦✦✦✦✦✦✦✦✦✦✦✦✦✦✦✦✦✦✦✦✦✦

90

Clef studies and transposition.

Alto clef.

428. Gregorian chant: Mass of Easter, Alleluia

429. Thibaut of Navarre: Trouvère song

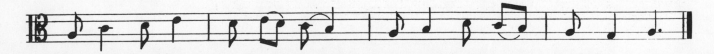

430. Handl (Gallus): Ecce concipies

431. Bach: Chorale prelude, Das alte Jahr vergangen ist

432. Bach: Cantata No. 151, alto aria

433. Mozart: String Quartet K.168

Andante

Clef studies and transposition.

434. Beethoven: String Quartet, Op. 59 No. 3

435. Franck: Symphony in d minor

436. Debussy: String Quartet

437. Bloch: Concerto Grosso

Allegro (♩ = 132)

f marcato

438. Hindemith: Sonata for Viola and Piano

Breit. Mit Kraft (♩ etwa 92)

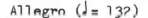

439. Hindemith: Sonata for Viola and Piano

Lebhaft (♩. bis 132)

94

Clef studies and transposition.

Tenor clef.

440. Anonymous (13th century, Manuscrit du Roi): Estampie Royal

441. Glareanus: Ninth ode of Horace

442. Victoria: O quam gloriosum

443. Altenburg: Nun laßt uns singen Gott dem Herrn

444. Bach: Cantata No. 154, tenor aria

445. Bach: Vom Himmel hoch, Variation IV

446. Beethoven: String Quartet, Op. 132

Clef studies and transposition.

447. Beethoven: String Quartet, Op. 59 No. 1

espress.

448. Brahms: Symphony No. 2 in D Major, Op. 73

449. Brahms: Trio in B Major, Op. 8, second version

450. Debussy: String Quartet

451. Hindemith: Konzertmusik für Streichorchester und Blechbläser

Soprano clef.

452. Plainsong (Bari Sequentiary): Prose on the holy relics of the
      Sainte-Chapelle

453. Schröter: Hört zu und seid getrost

454. Victoria: O quam gloriosum

Clef studies and transposition.

455. Bach: Cantata No. 151, soprano aria

Mezzo-soprano clef.

456. Gregorian chant: Mass of the fifth Sunday after Easter, Alleluia

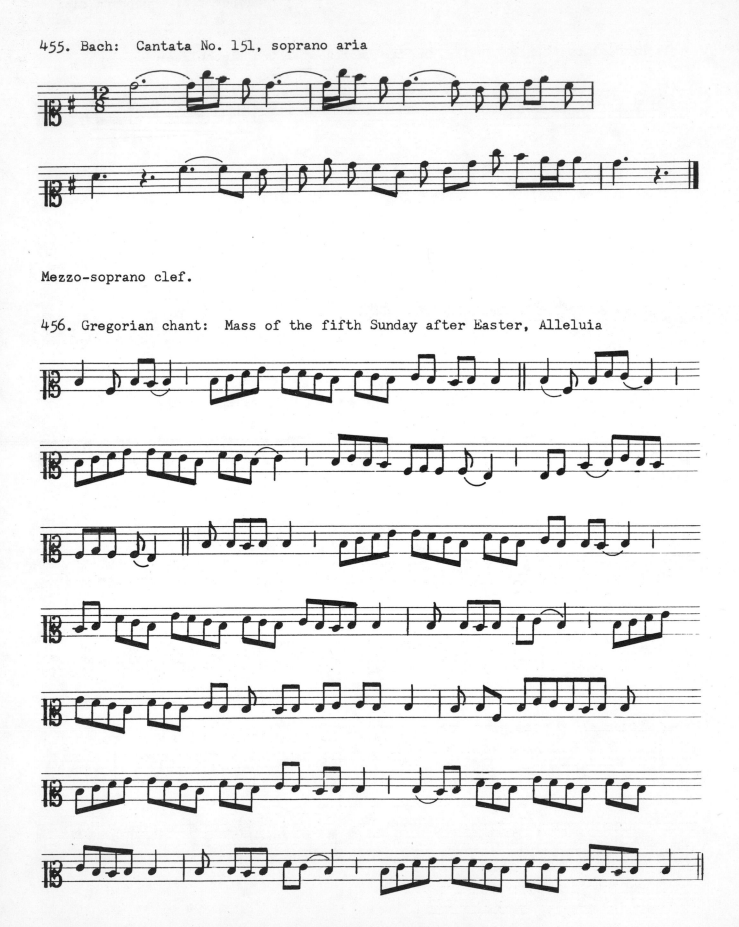

Mezzo-soprano clef. Baritone clef.

457. Byrd: Angelus Domini

Baritone clef.

458. Gregorian chant: Mass of Ember Wednesday after Pentecost, Post lectionem

Clef studies and transposition.

459. Gregorian chant: Mass of the fifth Sunday after Easter, Communion

460. Palestrina: O crux, ave, spes unica

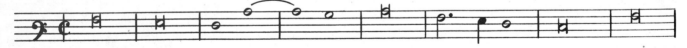

Mixed clefs.

461. Spervoghel: Minnelied

Mixed clefs.

462. Bach: Cantata No. 154, aria for alto and tenor

102

Clef studies and transposition.

463. Bach: Cantata No. 154, chorale

TRANSPOSITION

Suggested mode of performance: Sing at concert (sounding) pitch, naming the (concert) pitches sung with fixed-do solfège or letter names.

Practice suggestions:

1. Instruments in A sound a minor third lower than the written part. One way to effect this transposition is to substitute a soprano clef for the treble clef, move the key signature three in the sharp direction,[1] and raise all accidentals that appear before F, C, and G (on the soprano staff) one semitone.

2. Instruments in B-flat: Substitute a tenor clef for the treble clef, move the key signature two in the flat direction, and lower accidentals before B and E one half-step. (The actual sounding pitch, in the case of the clarinet and trumpet in B-flat, is an octave higher than that given by the tenor clef.)

3. Instruments in D: Substitute an alto clef for the treble clef, move the key signature two in the sharp direction, and raise accidentals before F and C a semitone. (D clarinets and trumpets sound an octave higher than the pitch given by the alto clef.)

4. Instruments in E-flat: Substitute a bass clef for the treble clef, move the key signature three in the flat direction, and lower accidentals before B, E, and A one half-step. (The horn in E-flat sounds an octave higher than the bass clef pitch; the E-flat clarinet and violino piccolo sound two octaves higher.)

5. Instruments in F: Substitute a mezzo-soprano clef for the treble clef, move the key signature one in the flat direction, and lower accidentals appearing before B one semitone.

6. Instruments in G: Substitute a baritone clef for the treble clef, move the key signature one in the sharp direction, and raise accidentals before F a semitone. Read the resulting pitches an octave higher.

****

Instruments in A.

464. Brahms: Symphony No. 2 (clarinet in A)

_____

[1]Even in music initially written without a key signature, the use of a signature as a transposition device is valid.

Clef studies and transposition.

465. Brahms: Symphony No. 3 (clarinet in A)

466. Rimsky-Korsakov: Sadko (clarinet in A)

467. Sibelius: Symphony No. 1 (clarinet in A)

468. Bernstein: The Age of Anxiety (clarinets in A)

Clef studies and transposition.

Instruments in B-flat.

469. Franck: Symphony in d minor (clarinet in B-flat and bassoon)

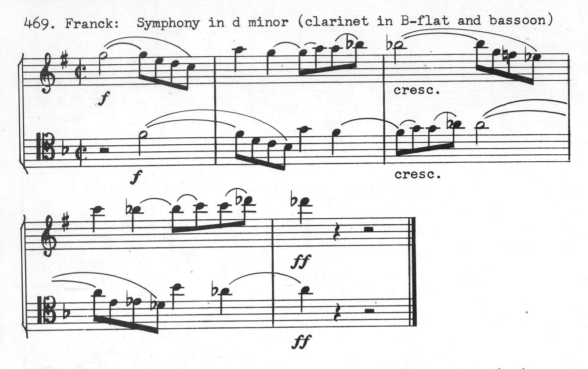

470. Brahms: Variations on a Theme by Joseph Haydn, Op. 56a (horn in B-flat)

471. Brahms: Symphony No. 1 (clarinet in B-flat)

472. Dvořàk: Slavonic Dance No. 4 (clarinet in B-flat)

Instruments in B-flat.

473. Sibelius: Vårsång (clarinet in B-flat)

cantabile

474. Casella: Serenata (clarinet in B-flat)

475. Hindemith: Sonata for Clarinet and Piano (clarinet in B-flat)

108

Clef studies and transposition.

476. Hindemith: Sonata for Clarinet and Piano (clarinet in B-flat)
Lebhaft (♩ bis 92)

Copyright © 1940 by B. Schott's Söhne, Mainz.

477. Aaron Copland: Quiet City (trumpet in B-flat)

Copyright 1941 by Aaron Copland; Renewed 1968.
Reprinted by permission of Aaron Copland and Boosey & Hawkes, Inc., Sole Licensees.

Instruments in D.

478. Bach: Suite No. 3 for Orchestra (trumpet in D)

479. Stravinsky: The Rite of Spring (trumpet in D)

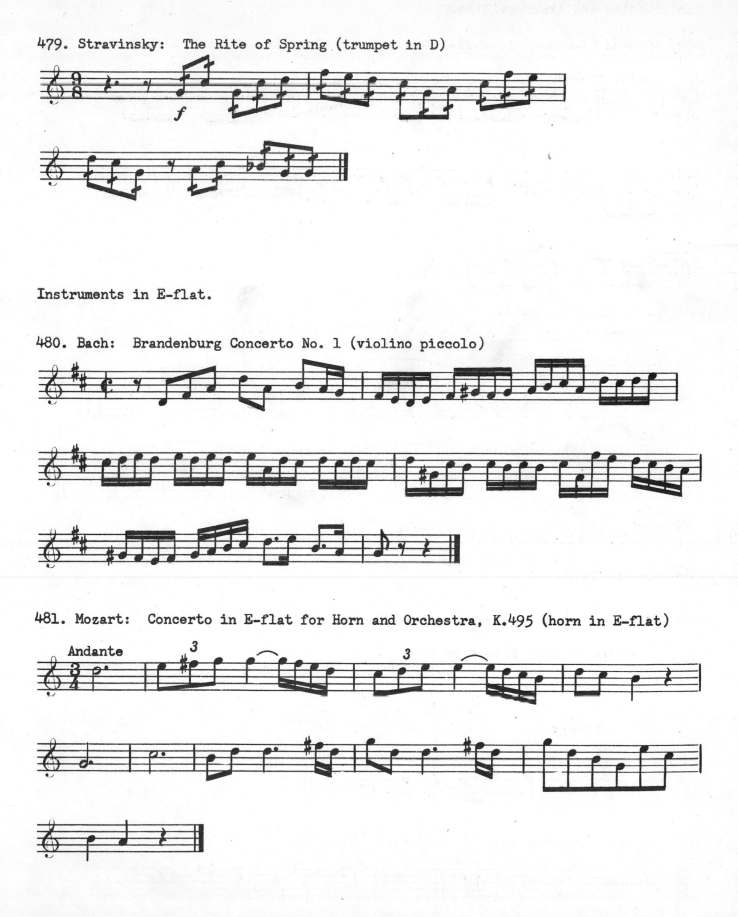

Instruments in E-flat.

480. Bach: Brandenburg Concerto No. 1 (violino piccolo)

481. Mozart: Concerto in E-flat for Horn and Orchestra, K.495 (horn in E-flat)

Clef studies and transposition.

482. Mozart: Concerto in E-flat for Horn and Orchestra (horn in E-flat)

Allegro vivace

483. Stravinsky: The Rite of Spring (clarinet in E-flat)

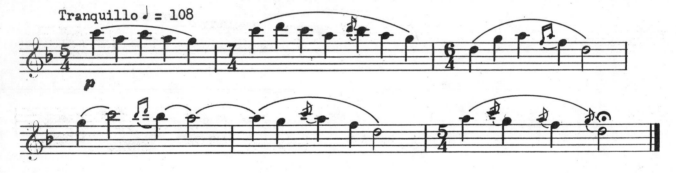

Tranquillo ♩ = 108

Instruments in F.

484. Franck: Symphony in d minor (English horn)

Tempo stretto come avanti

485. Mahler: Symphony No. 1 in d (horn in F)

486. Strauss: Don Quixote (horn in F)

487. Rimsky-Korsakov: Légende de la ville invisible de Kitej (alto flute in F)

488. Stravinsky: Firebird Suite (horn in F)

489. Griffes: The Pleasure Dome of Kubla Khan (English horn)

112

Clef studies and transposition.

490. Benjamin Britten: Serenade, Op. 31 (horn in F)

491. Creston: Two Choric Dances (horn in F)

Instruments in G.

492. Berlioz: Symphonie Funèbre et Triomphale, Apotheose

493. Stravinsky: The Rite of Spring (flute in G)

IV Examples from Literature

Suggested modes of performance:
1. Sing with fixed-do solfège.
2. Sing with letter names.
3. Sing with scale degree numbers (if appropriate).
4. Sing with movable-do solfège (if appropriate).
5. Sing on a neutral syllable.
6. Sing the text if one is provided. (In examples 508, 509, 510, and 530, one or more voices are to be considered untexted as only an incipit appears.)

****

*494. Ambrosian chant: Mass of Feast of St. James, Ingressa

Pu- er na- tus est no- bis, et fi- li-
-us da- tus est no- bis: cu- jus im-
-pe- ri- um su- per hu- me- rum e- jus: et

---

*In this chapter, an asterisk denotes a complete piece or movement.

114

12th century and earlier.

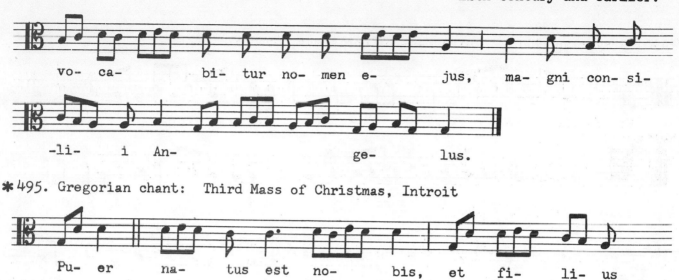

vo- ca- bi- tur no- men e- jus, magni con- si-

-li- i An- ge- lus.

* 495. Gregorian chant: Third Mass of Christmas, Introit

Pu- er na- tus est no- bis, et fi- li- us

da- tus est no- bis: cu- jus im-pe- ri- um

su- per hu- me- rum e- jus: et vo- ca-

-bi- tur no- men e- jus, ma- gni con- si- li-

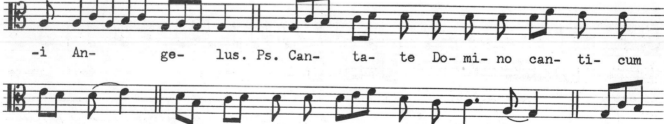

-i An- ge- lus. Ps. Can- ta- te Do- mi- no can- ti- cum

no- vum, qui a mi- ra- bi- li- a fe- cit. Glo-

-ri- a Pa- tri,et Fi- li- o, et Spi- ri- tu- i San- cto. Sic-

-ut e- rat in princi- pi- o, et nunc, et sem- per, et in

sae-cu- la sae- cu- lo- rum. A- men.

116

Examples from literature.

*496. Gregorian chant: Third Mass of Christmas, Gradual

Vi- de- runt o-   mnes fi- nes ter-   rae

sa- lu- ta-   re   De-   i

no- stri: ju- bi- la- te De-   o   o-

-mnis   ter- ra.

℣ No- tum fe- cit Do-

-mi- nus   sa- lu- ta-   re su-   um: an-te

con- spe- ctum gen- ti- um   re- ve-

-vit ju- sti-   ti- am   su- am.

497. Gregorian chant: Third Mass of Christmas, Alleluia

Al- le- lu- ia.   ij.[repeat]

℣ Di-   es san- cti-fi- ca- tus

il- lu- xit no-   bis: ve-

-ni- te gen- tes, et a- do- ra- te

Do- mi- num: qui-a ho- di- e   de- scen-

-dit lux ma-   gna su- per ter-

-ram.

498. Gregorian chant: Third Mass of Christmas, Offertory

Tu- i sunt cae- li, et tu- a est

ter-   ra: or- bem ter- ra- rum,

et ple- ni- tu- di- nem e-   jus

Examples from literature.

tu fun- da- sti: ju- sti- ti-

-a et ju- di- ci- um prae- pa-

-ra- ti- o se- dis

tu- ae.

*499. Gregorian chant: Third Mass of Christmas, Communion

Vi- de- runt o- mnes fi- nes ter- rae sa-

-lu- ta- re De- i no- stri.

* 500. Gregorian chant: Antiphon for Palm Sunday at the Solemn Procession

Pu- e- ri He- brae- o- rum ves- ti- men- ta pro- ster- ne-

-bant in vi- a, et cla- ma- bant di- cen- tes: Ho- san- na

fi- li- o Da- vid: be- ne- di- ctus qui ve- nit in no- mi-

-ne Do- mi- ni.

501. Gregorian chant: Mass of the fourth Saturday after Pentecost, Introit

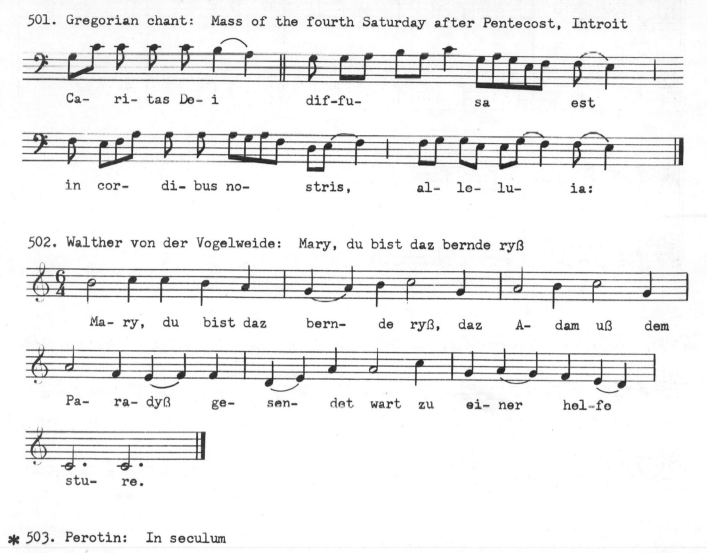

Ca- ri-tas De- i   dif-fu-   sa   est

in cor- di- bus no-   stris,   al- le- lu-   ia:

502. Walther von der Vogelweide: Mary, du bist daz bernde ryß

Ma- ry, du bist daz   bern- de ryß, daz A- dam uß dem

Pa- ra- dyß   ge- sen- det wart zu   ei- ner   hel=fe

stu- re.

* 503. Perotin: In seculum

In   se-

-cu-   lum

Examples from literature.

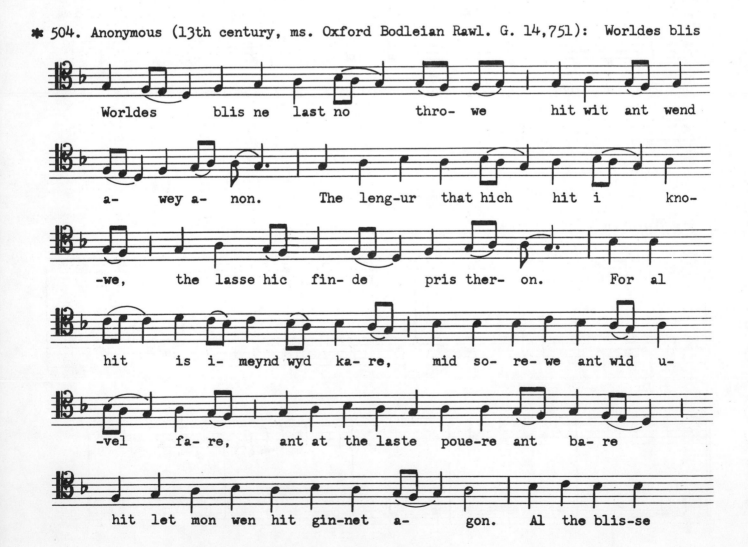

504. Anonymous (13th century, ms. Oxford Bodleian Rawl. G. 14,751): Worldes blis

13th century.

this he- re ant tho-re   bi- lou- keth at   hende   wop ant

mon.

* 505. Plainsong (Bari Sequentiary): Prose on the Holy Crown

Ver- bum bo- num et jo- cun- dum   Quod jo- cun-det to- tum mun-

-dum   Per os pu- rum   per cor mun- dum   Per- so- ne- mus ho- di-

-e.   Per quod mun-dum ve- ne- re- tur   Ve- ne- ra- tum col- lau-

-de- tur   Col- lau- da- tum ex- al- te- tur   Ser-tum re- gis glo-

-i- e.   A- ve ve- ri Sa- lo- mo- nis   Co- ro- na re-demp-

-ti- o- nis   Do- num cun- ctis ma- jus do- nis   Fran- co- rum pre-

-si-   di- um.   A- ve sa- crum ser- tum Christi   A- ve Chri-

-sto pla- cu- i- sti   A- ve Fran-cis con-tu- li- sti   De- cus et

Examples from literature.

im- pe- ri- um.   A- ve ser-tum dul- cis spi- ne   Pro-te-gentur

si- ne fi- ne   Per te re- ges et re- gi- ne   In fe- li- ci Fran-

-ci- a   Sup- pli- ca- mus sem- per ser- va   Re- gnum no- strum

et gu- ber- na   Nos- que trans-fer ad e- ter-na   Su- per-no-

-rum gau-di- a.   A- men.

506. Anonymous (13th century, Manuscrit du Roi): Estampie Real

* 507. Anonymous (13th century, Manuscrit du Roi): Danse Real

* 508. Anonymous (13th century, Le chansonnier de La Clayette): Trois sereurs seurs

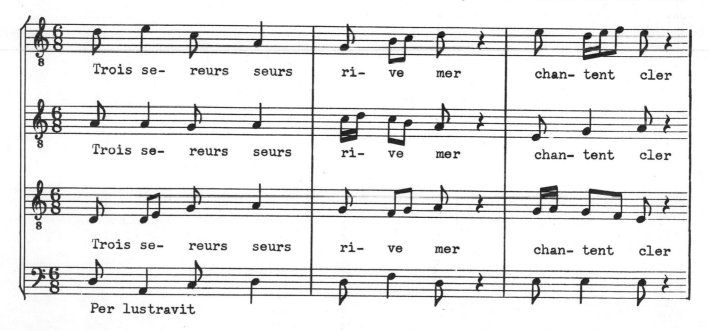

Trois se- reurs seurs   ri- ve mer   chan- tent cler

Trois se- reurs seurs   ri- ve mer   chan- tent cler

Trois se- reurs seurs   ri- ve mer   chan- tent cler

Per lustravit

124

Examples from literature.

la jo- ne- te   fu bru- ne- te   de brun a- mi

la mai- ne- e a- pe- le   Ro- bin son a-

l'ain-ne- [e] dit   [a] on doit   bien jo- ne

s'a-a-   ti   Je sui bru- ne   s'a- vrai brun a-

-mi   pri- se   m'a-vez el bois   ra- me re- por-

da- me a- mer   et s'a- mour   gar- der c'il

-mi au-   si.

-tez   mi.

qui   la.

Transcribed and edited by
James H. Cook. Used by
permission.

* 509. Anonymous (13th century, Codex Bamberg): Styrps regia/ Armonizans/ Amen

Styrps re- gi- a virgo Ma- ri- a,

Ar- mo- ni- zans can-ti- ca no- stra psal-

Amen

tu stel- la cla-ra ru- ti- la,

-lat mu- si- ca, ma- tri-cum sit u- ni-

tu pi- a ex- pi- a sce- le- ra,

-ca De- i- ca pa- rens at- que fi- li-

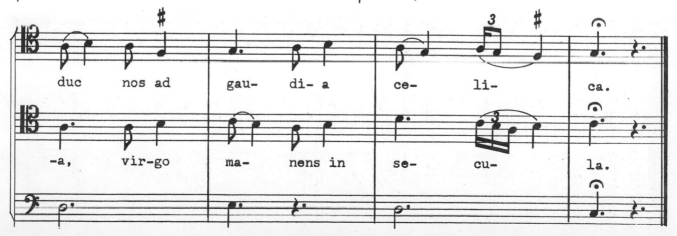

duc nos ad gau- di- a ce- li- ca.

-a, vir-go ma- nens in se- cu- la.

126

Examples from literature.

✱ 510. Anonymous (13th century, Codex Bamberg): In seculum breve

In seculum breve

13th century.

128

Examples from literature.

✱ 511. Gillebert de Berneville: Rotrouenge

De moi do- le-   reus vos chant   Je fui nez en

de- crois- sant   N'on- ques n'eu en   mon vi- vant

Deus bons jors.'   J'ai a   nom: Mes- che-ans d'a- mors.

✱ 512. Meister Alexander: Master-song

O we daz nach lie- be gat   leit so man ez tri- be.

Nu wil mynne unde   ist ir rat   daz ich da- von

scri- be.   Sie sprach sel- le wi- der mich

Scrib daz leyt ob al- len ley- de Swa sich heb von

he- be schey-de Tru-rich unde un- end- e-   lich.

513. Wizlaw von Rügen: Master-song

Ich par-   te- re dich durch mi- ne   vro- wen

de dich lep-lich sach vor mi- nen ou-   ghen.

* 514. Anonymous (14th century, Colmarer Liederhandschrift): Johannes der sach

* 515. Anonymous (14th century, ms. Oxford, Corpus Christi College 59): Edi beo thu

Examples from literature.

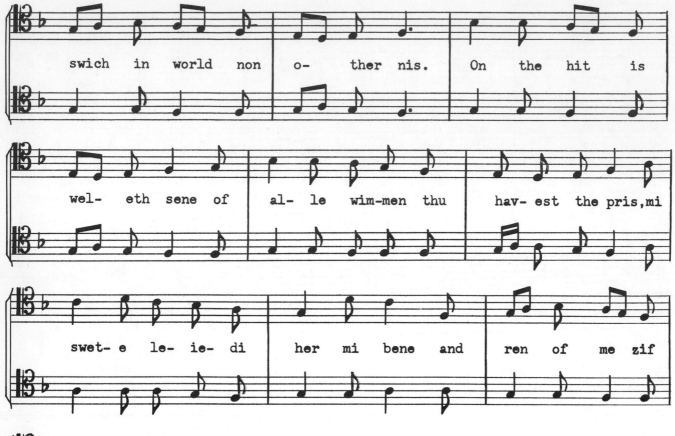

swich in world non o- ther nis. On the hit is

wel- eth sene of al- le wim-men thu hav-est the pris,mi

swet- e le- ie- di her mi bene and ren of me zif

thi wille is.

516. Anonymous (14th century, ms. British Museum Arundel 248): Bien duest chanter

Bien duest chan- ter ky eust lea- le

a- mi- e, Gar-re ter- roit ky bien la

seust choi- sir.

*517. Machaut: Virelai

He, da-me de vail- lan- ce, vo- stre dou-ce sam- -blan- ce m'a pris sans def-fi- an- ce, mais au pen- re sans lan- ce m'a nau-re du-re- ment.

1. -ment.

2. Fine

Car vo-stre dous ri- ant vair oueil et
Et vo-stre gra-ci- eus a- cueil plein

1. 2.

vo- stre sim- ple chie- re
de plai- sant ma- nie- re Ont

fait par leur puis- san- ce que m'a-mour m'espe- ran-

-ce, ma joi-e, ma plai- sen- ce, et tou-te ma fi-

D.C. al fine

-an- ce maint en vous seu-le- ment.

518. Machaut: Virelai

Li- e- ment me de- droit port
Que je sui au droit port

par sam- blant, mais je port sans
de mort sans nul de- port se

132

Examples from literature.

joie et sans de- port,
d'a- mours n'ay tel port u- qu'il
-ne si grief poin- tu- re
me pregne en sa cu-
1.
2.
-re.
Car quant de vo fi-
E- spris sui d'une ar-
-gu- re la dou- ce pour-trai- tu- re de
-su- re, ar- dant, cru- euse et su- re, plein-
1.
2.
dens mon cuer re- cort,
-ne de tout des- cort.

519. Muscatblut: Master-song

Got vat- ter worcht on al- le vorcht hym- mel und erd,

mensch-lich ge- berd und al- le cre- a- tu- re.

520. Ciconia: Dolce fortuna

Dol-

-ce, dol- ce for- tu-

-na

*521. Anonymous (early 15th century, Locheimer Liederbuch): Minnelied

All mein ge- den- ken die ich han, die sind bei dir.
Du aus- er- wel- ter ein- ger trost,bleib ster bei mir! Du, du, du solt an mich ge- den- ken; het ich

al- ler wunsch ge- walt, von dir wolt ich nicht

wen- ken.

*522. Anonymous (15th century, ms. Aosta): Crucifixum in carne

Cru- ci- fix- um
Cru- ci- fix- um

in car- ne
in car- ne

lau- da- te quem se- pul-
lau- da- te quem se- pul-

134

Examples from literature.

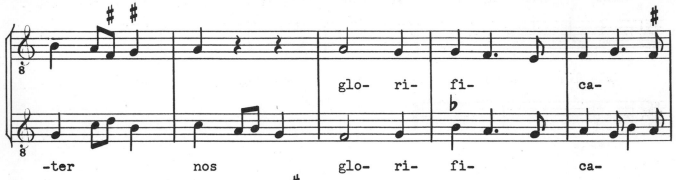

Transcribed and edited by Charles L. Turner. Used by permission.

523. Dufay: Missa Se la face ay pale, Kyrie

524. Dufay: Missa Se la face ay pale, Kyrie

Examples from literature.

525. Ockeghem: Missa Prolationum, Patrem

*526. Anonymous (late 15th century, ms. Paris BN fr. 12744): secular song

Gen- tils ga- lans de Fran-   ce,   Qui

a   la   guer- re   al-   lez, Je   vous pry qu'il vous

plai-   se   mon a- my sa-   lu- er.

527. Gafori: Example of triple proportion

528. Josquin: Missa Hercules dux Ferrariae, Agnus Dei

529. Isaac: Tota pulchra es

138

Examples from literature.

✱ 530. Anonymous (early 16th century, ms. Cappella Giulia XIII):   D'un altre amer

D'un altre amer

16th century.

Examples from literature.

✱ 531. Sachs: Master-song

Wo das Haus nit bau- et der Herr, so ar- bei- ten
al- le die dar- an bau- en sehr; wo nicht der Herr

um- son- ste sel- ber be- hu- ten ist die
durch Gun- ste

Stadt durch sein Bau- ung, Gut und Ge- nad' so wacht

um- sonst der Wäch- ter.

✱ 532. Grünewald: Mailied

Mir gliebt in grü- nen mei- en die fröh- lich

som- mer- zeit, in der sich thut er- freu- en die

gan- ze chri- sten- heit, und auch die liebst auf

er- den, die mir im her- zen leit.

✱ 533. Anonymous (16th century): Souterliedeken

534. Anonymous (16th century): Souterliedeken

535. Gaguinus: Setting of an elegiac poem

Car- mi-na   qui quon- dam stu-di- o   flo-

-ren-   te per-   e- gi Fle- bi- lis   heu moe-stos

co-   gor in- i-   re   Mo- dos.

142

Examples from literature.

536. Glareanus: Ode of Horace

Di- a- nam te- ne- rae di- ci- te Vir- gi- nes, In- ton- sum

pu- e- ri di- ci- te Cyn- thi- um La- to- nam- que su- pre-

-mo Di- le- ctam pe- ni- tus Jo- vi.

537. Glareanus: Setting of a Phalaecian poem

Po- scit vi- sceri- bus ci- bo- que sum- pto Quem lex cor- po- ris

im- be- cil- la po- scit Lau- dem lin- gua De-o Pa- tri re- pendat.

* 538. Anonymous (16th century): Secular song

* 539. Lassus: Beatus vir

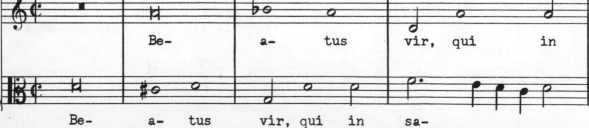

Be- a- tus vir, qui in

Be- a- tus vir, qui in sa-

16th century.

sa-   pi- en-   ti- a mo-
-pi- en-   ti- a mo-   ra-

-ra-   bi- tur,   et
-bi- tur,   et

qui   in   ju- sti-   ti-
qui in ju- sti-   ti- a me-

-a me-   di- ta- bi- tur,
-di- ta-   bi-

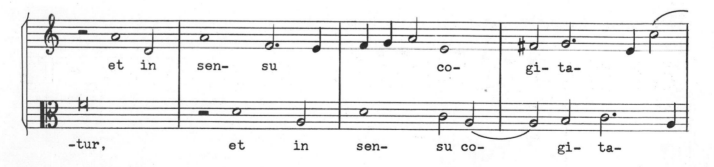

et in sen- su   co-   gi- ta-
-tur,   et in sen- su co-   gi- ta-

144

Examples from literature.

540. Handl (Gallus): Natus est nobis Deus

541. Byrd: Jhon come kisse me now

542. Byrd: The Carmans Whistle

543. Giles Farnaby: His Humour

Examples from literature.

544. Richard Farnaby: Fayne would I Wedd

* 545. Praetorius: Ein Kind geborn zu Bethlehem

Ein Kind ge- born zu Beth- le-

Ein Kind ge- born zu Beth- le-

-hem, Beth- le- hem, deß

-hem, Beth- le- hem, deß

freu- et sich Je- ru- sa- lem. Hal- le- lu-

freu- et sich Je- ru- sa- lem. Hal- le- lu-

-ja, Hal- le- lu- ja!

-ja, Hal- le- lu- ja!

546. Hassler: Ave maris stella

547. Guédron: Ballet de Madame

548. Schütz: Psalm 84

549. Monteverdi: L'incoronazione di Poppea

148

Examples from literature.

*550. White: Catch

551. Cavalli: Ercole Amante

Mor- mo- ra- te, o fiu- mi- cel- li, su- sur- ra- te, o
ven- ti cel- li,

552. Cesti: Il Pomo d'Oro

O gran Di- va de guer- rie- ri, Che pen-
-sie- ri Sve- gli in noi no- bi- li, e ca- sti, Se inse- gna- sti.

553. Biber: Sonata III for violin

554. Lully: Phaéton

555. Lully: Armide

Gravement

556. Purcell: Sarabande

150

Examples from literature.

557. Corelli: Sonata, Op. 5 No. 3

Adagio non troppo

558. Corelli: Sonata, Op. 5 No. 4
Adagio

559. Rameau: La Musette

L'ai-ma- ble Li- set- te For-me ces con- certs, Et sur sa mu-

-set- te Exprime et ré- pè- te Les plus ten- dres airs.

560. François Couperin: La Babet

Nonchalamment

561. Bach: Aria Variata alla Maniera Italiana

562. Bach: Aria Variata alla Maniera Italiana

563. Bach: Cantata No. 152

Doch se- lig ist ein aus- er-wähl- ter Christ,

der seinen Glau- bens- grund, der seinen Glau- bensgrund

auf die- sen Eck-stein le- get, weil er da- durch Heil

und Er- lö- sung fin- det, Er- lö- sung fin- det, weil er da-

-durch Heil und Erlö- sung, Heil und Er-lö- sung fin- det.

564. Bach: Cantata No. 153

Mein lieb- ster Gott, ach lass dich's doch er-

-bar- men, ach hilf doch, hilf mir Ar- men!

152

Examples from literature.

565. Bach: Cantata No. 153

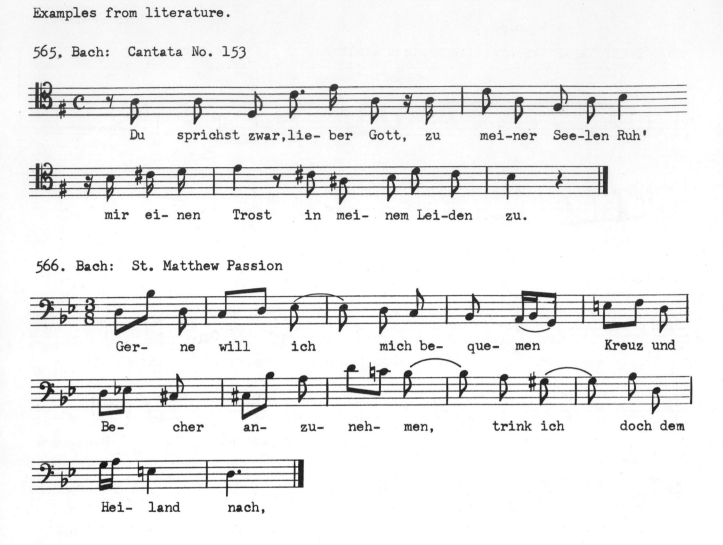

Du sprichst zwar, lie- ber Gott, zu mei-ner See-len Ruh'

mir ei- nen Trost in mei- nem Lei-den zu.

566. Bach: St. Matthew Passion

Ger- ne will ich mich be- que- men Kreuz und

Be- cher an- zu- neh- men, trink ich doch dem

Hei- land nach,

567. Bach: W.T.C., Book II, Fugue XXIII

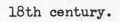

Examples from literature.

568. Telemann: Fantaisie No. 2

Presto

569. Domenico Scarlatti: Sonata in d minor, L. 413

Allegro.

570. Pergolesi: Stabat Mater

Sta- bat ma- ter do- lo-

Sta- bat ma- ter do- lo- ro-

-ro-   sa

571. Handel: Suite No. 5, Gigue

572. Handel: Aria

573. Handel: Concerto Grosso No. 1

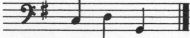

156

Examples from literature.

574. Handel: Jephtha

Pour forth no more un- heed- ed pray'rs

to I- dols deaf and vain, _____

575. Sammartini: Concerto for Violin and Orchestra

576. Stamitz: Sinfonia, Op. 5 No. 2

577. Gluck: Alceste

Lento

Per- se- pho- nens Ge- lei- te um -schwebet schon dein

18th century.

Haupt und for- dert sei- ne Beu- te! ja! dein Ge-
-mahl ge- ne- set, ja, dein Ge- mahl ge- ne- set; doch
dir winkt die Nacht.

578. Haydn: Symphony No. 8

579. Haydn: Symphony No. 44

Presto

580. Haydn: Piano Sonata (1778)

Molto vivace

p innocentemente

f

Examples from literature.

581. Haydn: Piano Sonata (1780)

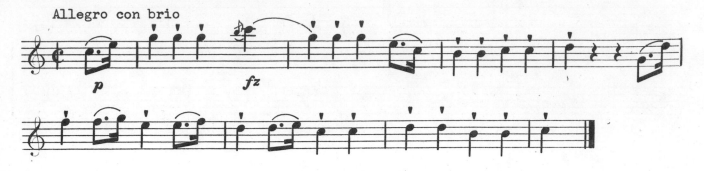

582. Haydn: Piano Sonata (1798)

*583. Pleyel: Duo for Two Violins, Op. 8 No. 1

584. Mozart: Benedictus sit Deus, K.117

quae di- stin- xe-   runt la- bi-a me-   a,quae

Examples from literature.

di- stin- xe-   runt la-

-bi-a   me-   a

585. Mozart: String Quartet No. 11, K.171

586. Mozart: Symphony No. 28, K.200

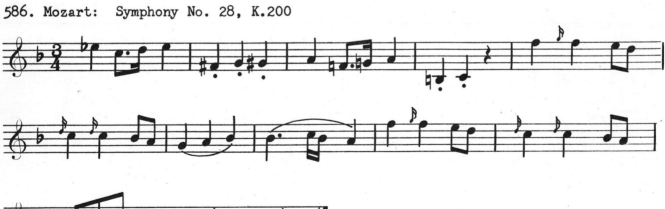

587. Mozart: Piano Sonata, K.282

588. Mozart: Piano Sonata, K.311

589. Mozart: Piano Sonata, K.332

590. Mozart: Vesperae Solennes de Confessore, K.339

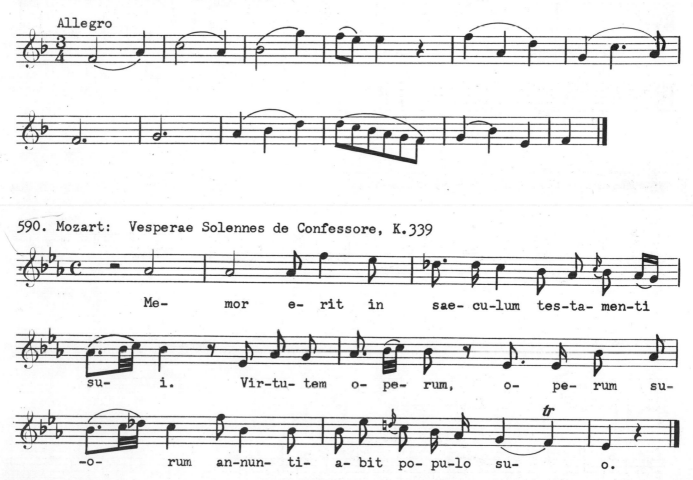

162

Examples from literature.

591. Mozart: Phantasie, K.475

592. Mozart: String Quartet No. 20, K.499

593. Mozart: Piano Sonata, K.545

594. Mozart: Così fan tutte, K.588

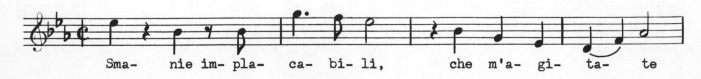

Sma- nie im- pla- ca- bi- li,   che m'a- gi- ta- te

18th century.

en- tro quest' a- ni- ma più non ces-
-sa- te, fin- chè l'an- go- scia mi fa mo-
-rir, mi fa mo- rir.

595. Mozart: Così fan tutte, K.588

Andante cantabile

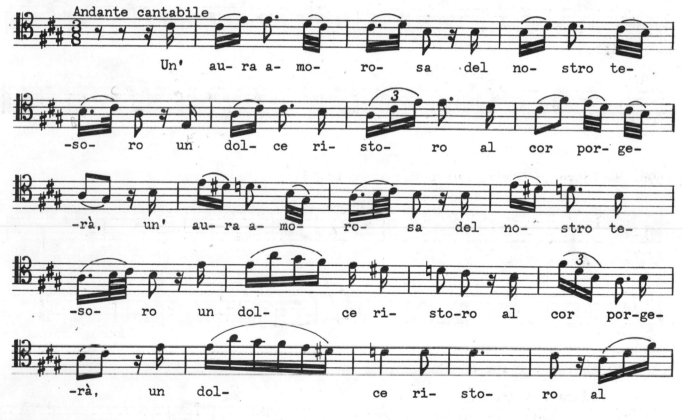

Un' au- ra a- mo- ro- sa del no- stro te-
-so- ro un dol- ce ri- sto- ro al cor por- ge-
-rà, un' au- ra a- mo- ro- sa del no- stro te-
-so- ro un dol- ce ri- sto- ro al cor por- ge-
-rà, un dol- ce ri- sto- ro al

cor por- ge- rà.

Examples from literature.

596. Beethoven: Sonata for Violin and Piano, Op. 12 No. 1

597. Beethoven: Piano Sonata, Op. 13

598. Beethoven: String Quartet, Op. 18 No. 5

599. Beethoven: Piano Sonata, Op. 31 No. 3

600. Beethoven: String Quartet, Op. 59 No. 1

601. Beethoven: String Quartet, Op. 59 No. 2

602. Beethoven: Fidelio, Op. 72

O wär' ich schon mit dir ver- eint, und dürf- te Mann dich nen- nen! Ein Mäd- chen darf ja, was es meint, zur Hälf- te nur be- ken- nen.

166

Examples from literature.

603. Beethoven: Piano Sonata, Op. 81a

604. Beethoven: Piano Sonata, Op. 90

Nicht zu geschwind und sehr singbar vorgetragen

605. Beethoven: Piano Sonata, Op. 101

Vivace alla Marcia

606. Beethoven: Piano Sonata, Op. 106

168

Examples from literature.

607. Beethoven: String Quartet, Op. 131

Ritmo di due battute

608. Beethoven: String Quartet, Op. 132

609. Beethoven: String Quartet, Op. 132

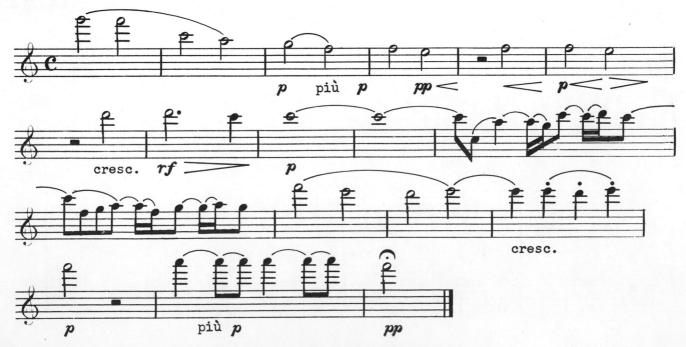

610. Schubert: Die schöne Müllerin, Op. 25, Wohin?

Ich hört' ein Bäch-lein rau- schen wohl aus dem

Fel- sen- quell, hin- ab zum Tha- le rau-

-schen so frisch und wun- der- hell.

611. Schubert: Die Schöne Müllerin, Op. 25, Am Feierabend

Hatt' ich tau- send Ar- me zu rüh- ren, könnt' ich

brau-send die Rä- der füh- ren, könnt' ich we- hen durch

al- le Hai- ne, könnt' ich dre- hen al- le Stei-ne,

dass die schö- ne Mül- le- rin merk- te mei- nen

treu- en Sinn, dass die schö- ne Mül- le-rin

merk- te mei- nen treu- en Sinn.

Examples from literature.

612. Schubert: Quintet, Op. 163

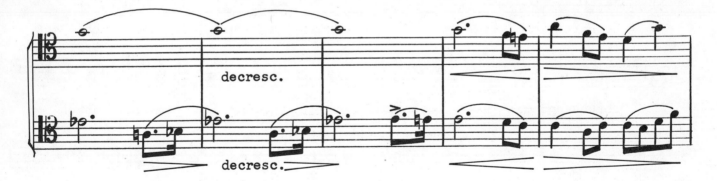

613. Schubert: Symphony No. 7, Op. posthumous

614. Schubert: Symphony No. 7, Op. posthumous

615. Mendelssohn: Fingal's Cave, Op. 26

Examples from literature.

616. Mendelssohn: Symphony No. 3, Op. 56
Andante con moto M.M. ♩ = 72

617. Chopin: Etude, Op. 10 No. 3
Lento, ma non troppo (♩ = 100)

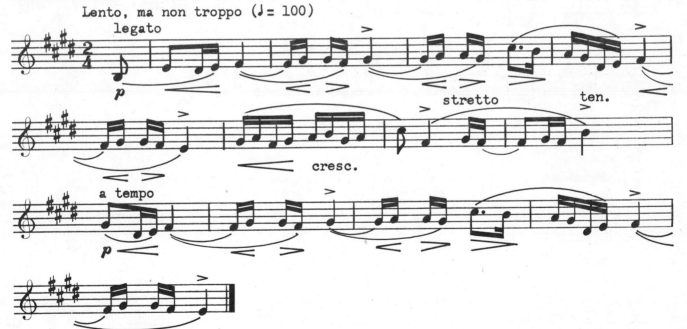

618. Chopin: Etude, Op. 10 No. 6
Andante (♩. = 69)

619. Chopin: Nocturne, Op. 15 No. 3

620. Chopin: Piano Sonata, Op. 35

621. Schumann: Liederkreis, Op. 39, Schöne Fremde

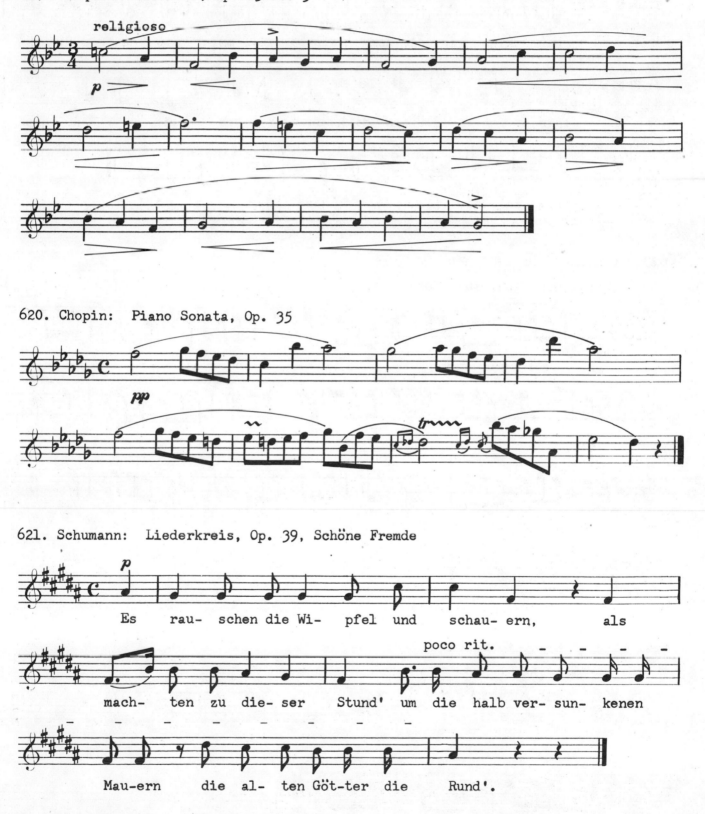

Es   rau- schen die Wi- pfel und   schau- ern,   als

mach- ten zu die- ser   Stund'   um die halb ver- sun- kenen

Mau- ern   die al- ten Göt- ter die   Rund'.

174

Examples from literature.

622. Schumann: Frauenliebe und Leben, Op. 42, Der Ring

Du Ring an mei- nem Fin- ger, mein gol- de- nes Rin-ge-

-lein, ich drü-cke dich fromm an die Lip- pen, dich

fromm an die Lip- pen, an das Her- ze mein!

623. Schumann: Ball-Scenen, Op. 109

Belebt, doch nicht zu rasch

624. Liszt: Mephisto Waltz

625. Wagner: Tannhäuser

Noch blei- be denn un- aus- ge- spro- chen dein süß Ge-

-heim- nis kur- ze Frist; der Zau- ber

blei- be un- ge- bro- chen, bis du der Lö- sung

mäch- tig bist, bis du der Lö- sung, der Lö- sung

mäch- tig bist.

626. Wagner: Das Rheingold

Dem Haupt fügt sich der Helm: ob sich der

(sehr leise)

Zau- ber auch zeigt? "Nacht und Ne- bel,

nie- mand gleich!"

Examples from literature.

627. Verdi: Rigoletto

628. Brahms: Piano Sonata, Op. 5

629. Brahms: Piano Sonata, Op. 5

630. Brahms: Piano Trio, Op. 8

631. Brahms: Variations on a Hungarian Song, Op. 21 No. 2

Allegro

632. Brahms: Horn Trio, Op. 40

dolce

poco cresc.   dim.

Examples from literature.

633. Brahms: Variations on a Theme by Joseph Haydn, Op. 56b

634. Brahms: Piano Trio, Op. 87

635. Brahms: Clarinet Quintet, Op. 115

636. Grieg: Piano Concerto, Op. 16

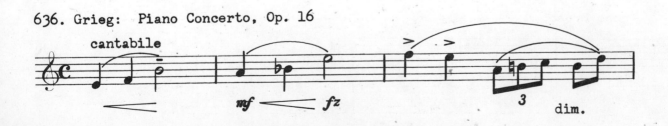

poco ritard.

637. Mussorgsky: Pictures at an Exhibition, Samuel Goldenberg and Schmuyle
   Andante

638. Dvořák: Slavonic Dance No. 1, Op. 46 No. 1

639. Dvořák: Slavonic Dance No. 2, Op. 46 No. 1

180

Examples from literature.

640. Tchaikovsky: Symphony No. 4, Op. 36

641. Tchaikovsky: Symphony No. 5, Op. 64

642. Glazunov: Symphony No. 3

643. Chausson: Poème, Op. 25

644. Rimsky-Korsakov: Légende de la ville invisible de Kitej

645. Fauré: Pièces Brèves, Op. 84, Capriccio

Andante quasi Allegretto ♩.= 96

dolce

poco a poco cresc.

mf

p

646. Granados: Danzas Españolas, Villanesca

182

Examples from literature.

647. Ives: Lincoln, the Great Commoner

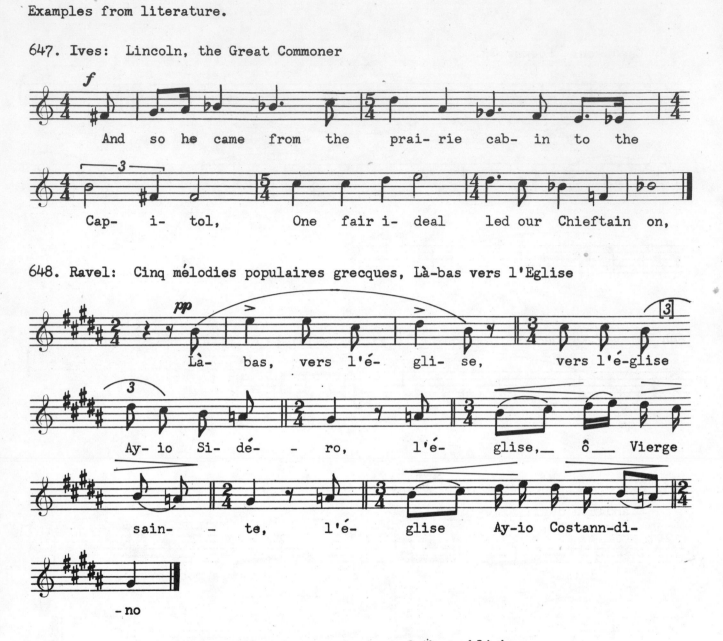

648. Ravel: Cinq mélodies populaires grecques, Là-bas vers l'Eglise

649. Ravel: Cinq mélodies populaires grecques, Chanson des cueilleuses de lentisques

650. Griffes: The Pleasure Dome of Kubla Khan

p lontano

Copyright, 1920, by G. Schirmer. Reprinted by permission.

651. Hába: String Quartet No. 1, Op. 4

Andante cantabile

Copyright 1936. Universal Edition.
Used by permission of the publisher.
Theodore Presser Company. Sole representative.
USA, Mexico, and Canada.

652. Nielsen: Maskarade

Fǿrst kom- mer fael og   fus   Mon- sǿr Je- ro- ni-   mus:

Examples from literature.

"Tvi dig, du sul- ten Lus! Du, som i Sus og

Dus ø- der din Fa- ders Krus paa en ge- men Kan-tus-

-se som du i en Rus traf paa et Jom-fru- hus_____

Copyright © 1946 by Wilhelm Hansen Musik-Forlag. Reprinted by permission.

653. Wellesz: Alkestis

Ihr be- tet, be- tet,a- ber sehr um- sonst. Dies Weib

geht heut hin-ab in Ha- des Haus mit mir.

Copyright 1936. Universal Edition.
Used by permission of the publisher.
Theodore Presser Company. Sole representative.
USA, Mexico, and Canada.

654. Bloch: Baal Shem (Three Pictures of Chassidic Life), Vidui

Copyright MCMXXIV by Carl Fischer Inc., New York. International Copyright
Secured. Copyright Renewed. Used by permission of Carl Fischer, Inc.

655. Bloch: Concerto Grosso

656. Schoenberg: Concerto for Violin and Orchestra, Op. 36

657. Schoenberg: Concerto for Violin and Orchestra, Op. 36

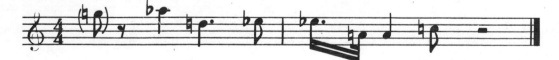

658. Schoenberg: Fourth String Quartet, Op. 37

Examples from literature.

659. Schoenberg: Fourth String Quartet, Op. 37

660. Webern: Langsamer Satz for String Quartet

661. Webern: Langsamer Satz for String Quartet

662. Webern: Vier Lieder für Gesang und Orchester, Op. 13

663. Webern: Vier Lieder für Gesang und Orchester, Op. 13

Examples from literature.

664. Webern: Cantata, Op. 29

Zün-   den- der   Licht-blitz   des   Le-   bens

schlug   ein   aus der Wol-   ke   des

Wor-   tes.

665. Berg: Violin Concerto

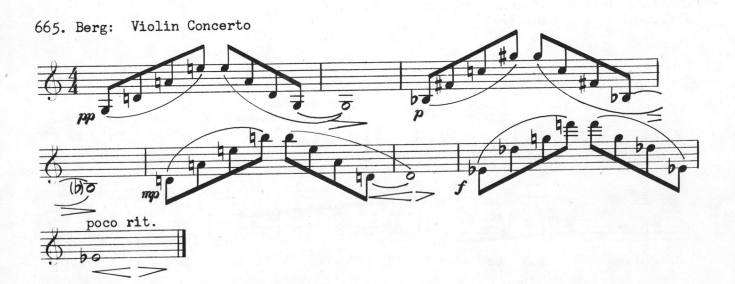

666. Berg: Violin Concerto

pp ma espr.

667. Hindemith: Konzertmusik für Streichorchester und Blechbläser

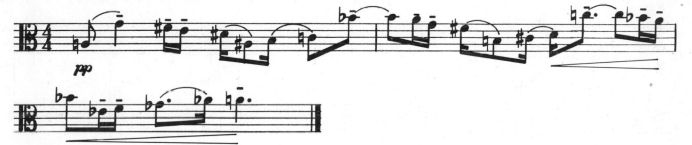

pp

668. Hindemith: Mathis der Maler

mf

Son- ni-ges Land, mil- des Drän- gen schon

na-hen Som-mers; das er- regt und betäubt zu- gleich.

Leicht er- ste- hen Plä- ne und Ta- ten, fast wie in

Examples from literature.

jun- gen Jah- ren. Wo sonst trü- be Schat- ten hän- gen,

ist rings- um al- les Sein im Licht be- wegt.

669. Hindemith: Mathis der Maler

Wieder lebhafter

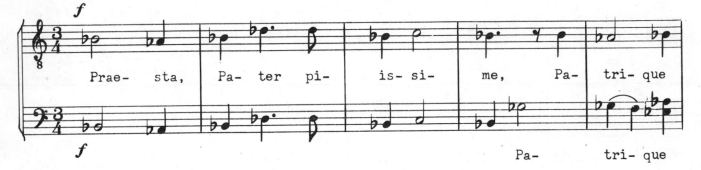

Prae- sta, Pa- ter pi- is- si- me, Pa- tri- que

Pa- tri- que

com- par U- ni- ce, cum Spi- ri- tu Pa-

com- par Pa-

-ra- -cli- to, _____ re- gnans per

-ra- -cli- to, _____

o- mne   sae- cu-   lum.

670. Hindemith: Sinfonische Metamorphosen

671. Hindemith: Sinfonische Metamorphosen

192

Examples from literature.

672. Hindemith: Sinfonische Metamorphosen

673. Hindemith: Neues vom Tage

... steht das   Wohl   des   Volks auf dem   Spiel.

674. Hindemith: Neues vom Tage

Es   er- scheint uns   gänz- lich   ü - ber- flüs-

-sig, daß   wir zu- sam- men   blei- ben.

675. Béla Bartók: Concerto for Orchestra

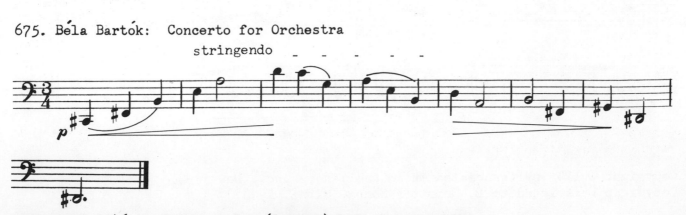

stringendo

676. Béla Bartók: Concerto for Orchestra

Andante, non troppo, ♩ = 73-64

677. Béla Bartók: Concerto for Orchestra

678. Béla Bartók: Concerto for Orchestra

Poco agitato, mosso,
molto rubato, ♩ = ca 80

f, molto espr. legato

poco rallent. -

194

Examples from literature.

679. Zoltán Kodály: Missa Brevis

Qui tol- lis pec- ca- ta mun- di, mi- se- -re- re no- bis.

Copyright 1947, 1951 by Boosey & Hawkes, Inc.
Reprinted by permission.

680. Zoltán Kodály: Missa Brevis

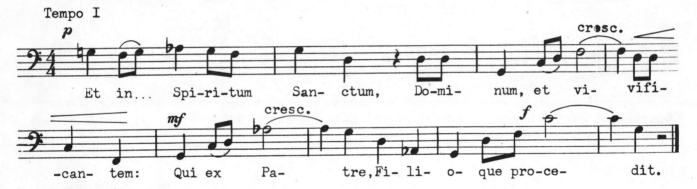

Et in... Spi-ri-tum San-ctum, Do-mi- num, et vi- vifi--can- tem: Qui ex Pa- tre,Fi- li- o- que pro-ce- dit.

Copyright 1947, 1951 by Boosey & Hawkes, Inc.
Reprinted by permission.

681. Stravinsky: Symphony of Psalms

Copyright 1931 by Edition Russe de Musique; Renewed 1958.
Copyright and Renewal assigned to Boosey & Hawkes, Inc.
Revised Edition Copyright 1948 by Boosey & Hawkes, Inc.
Reprinted by permission.

682. Stravinsky: Symphony of Psalms

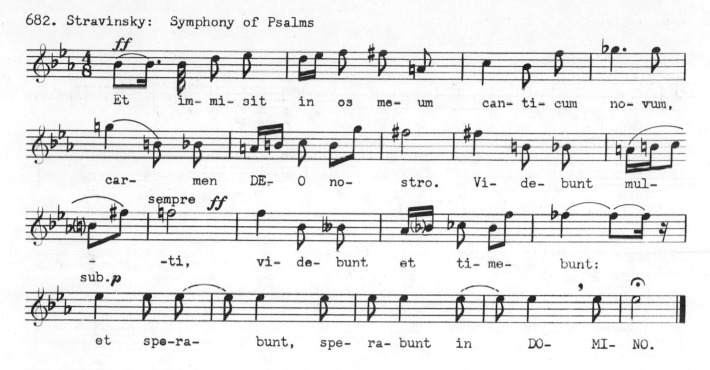

Et im-mi-sit in os me-um can-ti-cum no-vum, car-men DE- O no- stro. Vi- de- bunt mul- -ti, vi- de- bunt et ti-me- bunt: et spe-ra- bunt, spe-ra-bunt in DO- MI- NO.

683. Stravinsky: Symphony in C

684. Stravinsky: Symphony in C

196

Examples from literature.

685. Stravinsky: Symphony in C

Largo ♩ = 50

686. Igor Stravinsky: The Rake's Progress

♩ = 56

If   boys   had   wings___   and   girls   had   stings

And   gold___   fell   from   the   sky,_____   If

new___ laid eggs wore wood- en legs

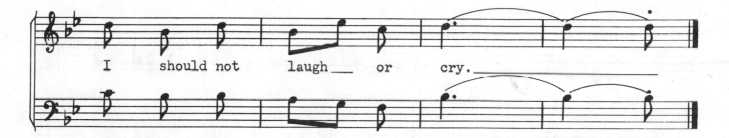

I should not laugh___ or cry.____

687. Igor Stravinsky: The Rake's Progress

Al- ways the quar- ry___ that I stalk Fades___ or e-

-vades me, and_ I walk___ An end- less hall of chande-

-liers In light that blinds, in light that sears,____ Re-

-flec- ted from___ a mil- lion smiles____ All emp-

-ty as the coun- try miles Of sil- ly wood and sense-

Examples from literature.

-less park;   And on — — ly in my   heart the dark.

688. Stravinsky: Threni

In- — ci- — pit, in- ci- pit la-

-men- ta- ti- o   Je- re- mi- ae   Pro- phe-

— -tae. . . . .

689. Stravinsky: Threni

Mesto ♩ = 46

Plo- rans   plo- ra- vit,   plo-ra-

Plo- rans   plo- ra- vit,   plo-ra-

-vit, plo- ra- vit in   noc- te,   et la-

-vit,   plo- ra- vit in   noc- te,   et la-

20th century.

-cry- mae e- jus . . . . in . . . . ma- xil-

-cry- mae e- jus in . . . ma- xil-lis

-lis e- jus.

e- - jus.

690. Aaron Copland: The Tender Land

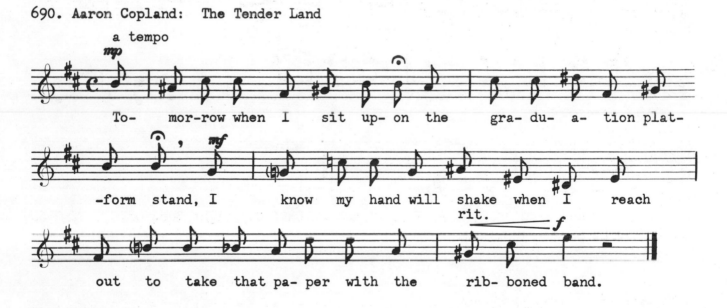

To- mor-row when I sit up- on the gra- du- a- tion plat-

-form stand, I know my hand will shake when I reach

out to take that pa- per with the rib- boned band.

Examples from literature.

691. Aaron Copland: The Tender Land

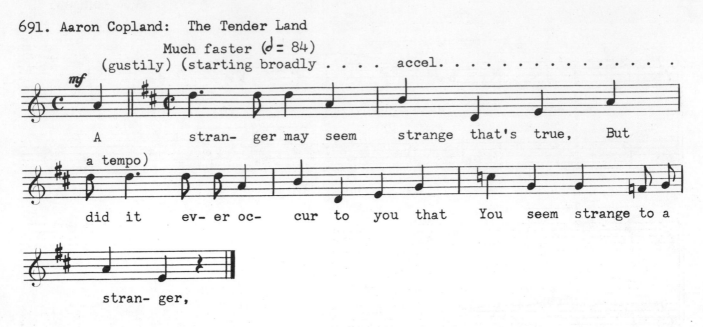

Copyright 1954 by Aaron Copland.
Reprinted by permission of Aaron Copland and Boosey & Hawkes, Inc., Sole Licensees.

692. Barber: First Symphony

Copyright, 1943, by G. Schirmer, Inc. International Copyright Secured.
Reprinted by permission.

693. Barber: First Symphony

20th century.

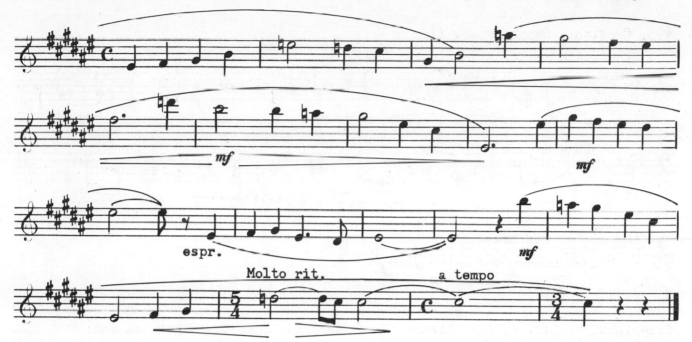

694. Menotti: The Saint of Bleeker Street

They come up the bend- ing road in gold- en ar- mor, the

sol- diers, and a- mong them a purple cloak. My

Je- sus! How large a cross for one man to bear! Dust in His mouth

and salt of bit- ter tears. His cheeks rib-boned with blood

shed by the sharp and cru- el crown.

202

Examples from literature.

695. Creston: Symphony No. II

Slow--with deep emotion ♩.= 40

696. Creston: Symphony No. II

expressively

697. Foss: The Jumping Frog of Calaveras County

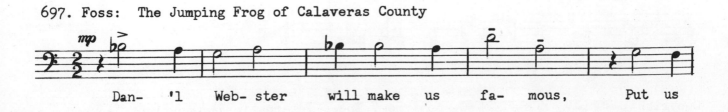

Dan- 'l Web- ster will make us fa- mous, Put us

20th century.

all on the map he will!_____ If we brag a bit,

who can blame us? Ain't man-y frogs with his

jump- ing skill,

698. Foss: Song of Anguish

Every one_____ that is found shall be thrust through

and eve- ry one_____ that is joined un- to them shall

fall by the sword _____

699. Mennin: String Quartet No. 2

Examples from literature.

700. Chou Wen-Chung: Seven Poems of T'ang Dynasty

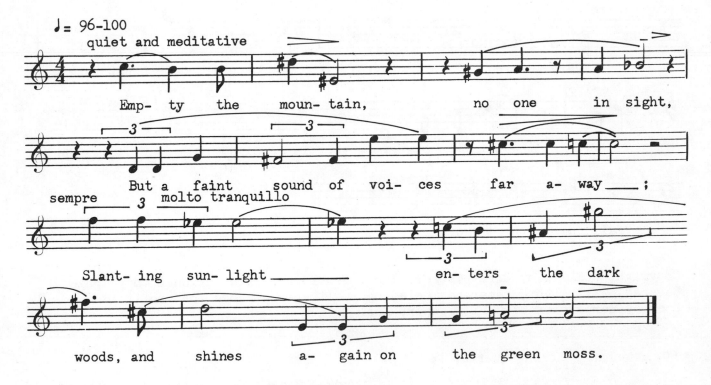

701. Dallapiccola: Volo di Notte

meno *f*; disinvolto

Ma cer- to!   Voi ver- re- te con me;   brinde-

-re- mo al vo- stro co- raggio,   al vo- stro va- lo- re...

quasi dolce

ed al- la no- stra a- mi- ci- zia.

702. Kabalevsky: Piano Concerto No. 3, Op. 50

mp cantando

703. Egk: Variationen über ein karibisches Thema

Moderato ♩ = 56

mp molto
cantabile

Examples from literature.

704. Tippett: A Child of Our Time

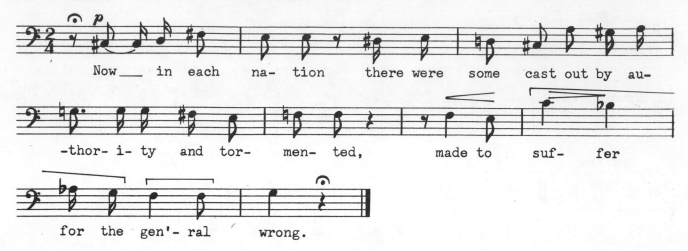

Now__ in each na- tion there were some cast out by au- -thor- i- ty and tor- men- ted, made to suf- fer for the gen'- ral wrong.

705. Tippett: A Child of Our Time

Allegro molto (♩ = 168-176)

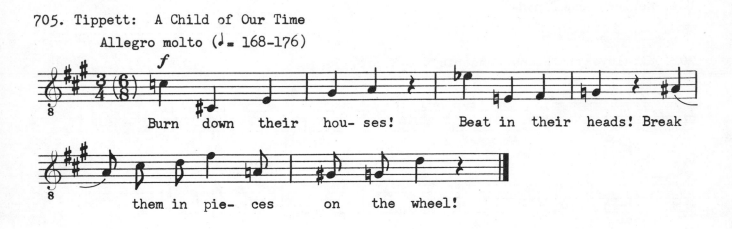

Burn down their hou- ses! Beat in their heads! Break them in pie- ces on the wheel!

706. Tippett: A Child of Our Time

I am caught be- tween my de- sires and their frus- -tra- tion as be- tween the ham- mer and the an- vil.

707. Benjamin Britten: Serenade, Op. 31

708. Benjamin Britten: Peter Grimes

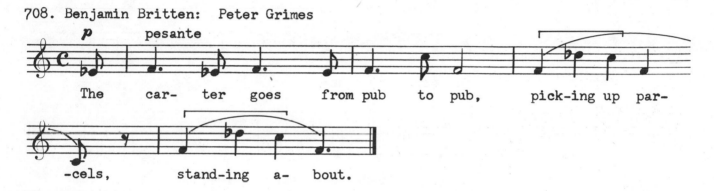

709. Benjamin Britten: Peter Grimes

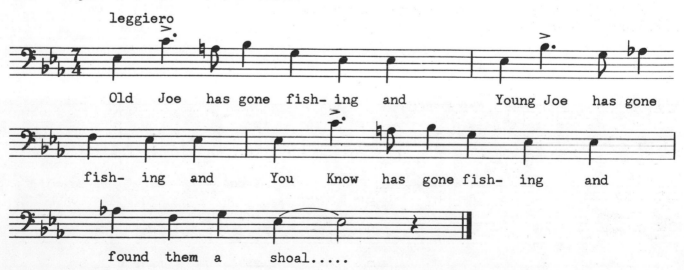

Examples from literature.

710. Benjamin Britten: War Requiem

711. Benjamin Britten: War Requiem

20th century.

sor- row ful to hear.____

712. Benjamin Britten: War Requiem

Li- ber scrip- tus pro- fe- re- tur, in quo to- tum con-

-ti- ne- tur, Un- de mun- dus ju- di- ce- tur.

713. Chavez: Concerto for Violin and Orchestra

tenuto

Examples from literature.

★ 714. Ginastera: 12 American Preludes, Sadness

715. Crumb: Ancient Voices of Children

V *Supplementary Materials*

INTERVALLIC CONSTRUCTION

Analyze the intervallic content of the following exercises, then sing them using letter names or fixed-do solfège.

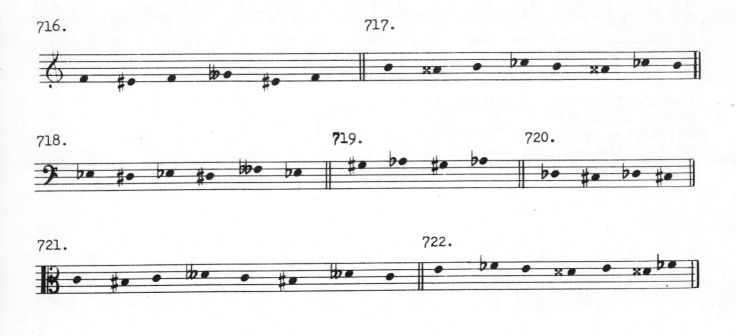

Sing the following interval chains, using letter names or fixed-do solfège to name the pitches sung. (Do not write out the pitches on the staff.)

Intervallic construction.

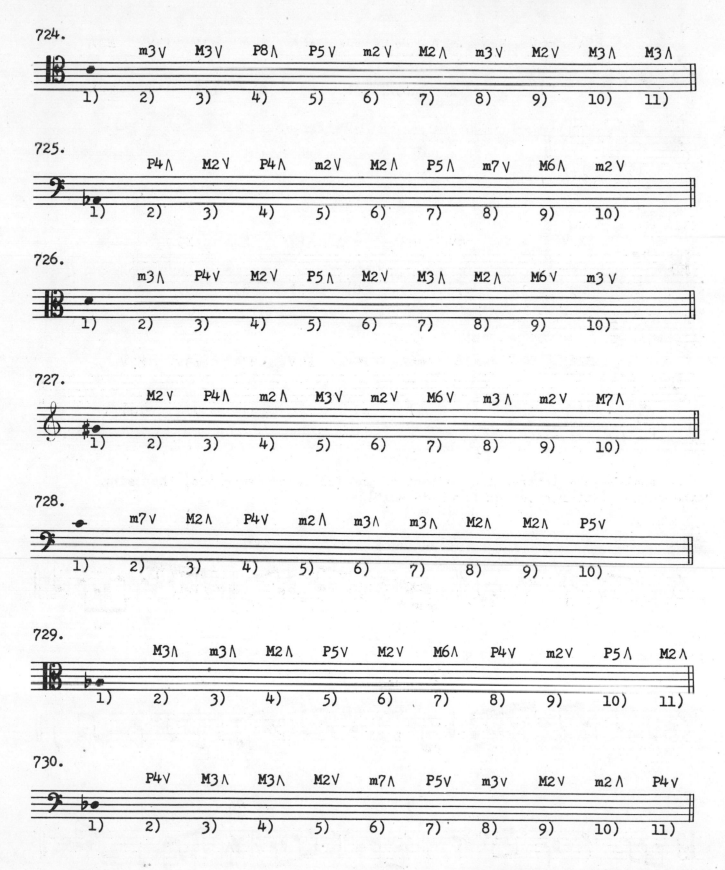

Supplementary materials.

731.

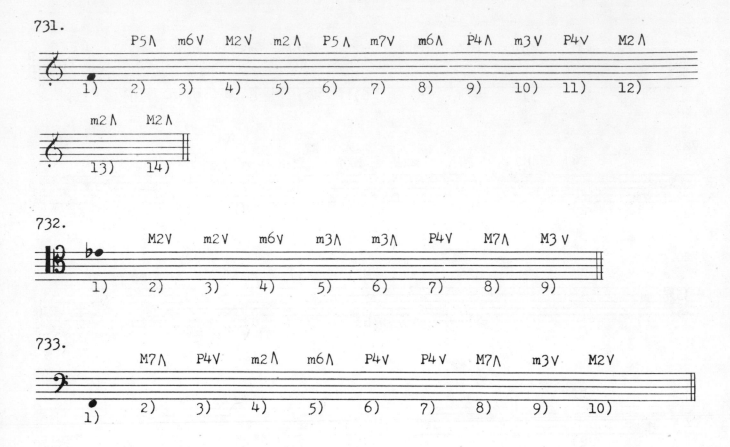

732.

733.

Analyze the intervallic content of the following exercises, then sing them using letter names or fixed-do solfège.

734.   735.   736.

737.   738.   739.

740.   741.   742.

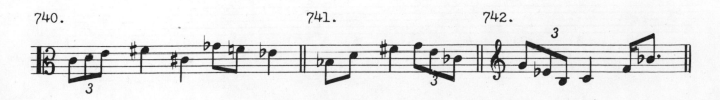

Intervallic construction.

743.

744.

745.

746.

747.

748.

749.

750.

751.

752.

753.

754.

755.

756.

757.

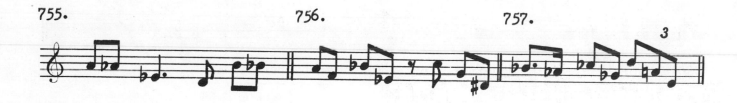

758.

759.

760.

761.

762.

763.

216

Supplementary materials.

764.   765.   766.

767.   768.   769.

770.   771.   772.

    Sing the following twelve-tone rows, then sing the inversion, the retrograde, and the retrograde inversion. Sing also several different transpositions of each form of the row. Use fixed-do solfège or letter names.

773. Schoenberg: Concerto for Violin and Orchestra, Op. 36

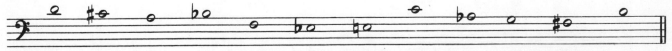

Copyright, 1939, by G. Schirmer, Inc. Reprinted by permission.

774. Schoenberg: Fourth String Quartet, Op. 37

Copyright, 1939, by G. Schirmer, Inc. International Copyright Secured. Reprinted by permission.

    Sing the following two examples. In each case, abstract the row and then proceed as above.

Intervallic construction.   Formal construction.

775. Korte: Alternate Rows I
Broadly expressive

776. Korte: Alternate Rows II
Quickly

FORMAL CONSTRUCTION

The task of sight-singing can be simplified if one is aware of the form of a piece, of pitch or rhythm patterns that recur. Sing the bracketed portions of each exercise and then the complete example.

It will be evident that observing similar relationships will facilitate reading many of the examples in the preceding chapters.

777. Beethoven: String Quartet, Op. 59 No. 1
Allegro

Supplementary materials.

778. Brahms: Symphony No. 2, Op. 73

pp sempre

779. Stravinsky: Firebird Suite

REDUCTION

The two examples below illustrate the possibility of reducing a complex melodic line to a simpler form which reveals the underlying stepwise motion. Sing the reduction and then the original melody in each case.

Awareness of such an underlying structure frequently can facilitate the sight-singing process.

780. Mozart: String Quartet, K.428

Reduction. Counterpoint in two voices.

781. Sibelius: Symphony No. 2, Op. 43

COUNTERPOINT IN TWO VOICES

   In the following section, the arabic figures above the staff indicate intervals above the cantus firmus; figures below the staff indicate intervals below the cantus firmus.

   Play the cantus firmus and sing the added voice, using letter names, solfège, or scale degree numbers, or perform each example similarly as an ensemble drill. (Do not write out the counterpoint.)

First species.

782. Fux: Gradus ad Parnassum

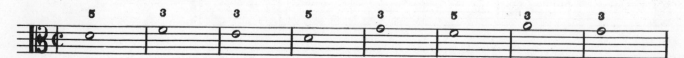

Supplementary materials.

783. Fux: Gradus ad Parnassum

Second species.

784. Fux: Gradus ad Parnassum

785. Fux: Gradus ad Parnassum

Third species.

786. Fux: Gradus ad Parnassum

787. Fux: Gradus ad Parnassum

Fourth species.

788. Fux: Gradus ad Parnassum

222

Supplementary materials.

789. Fux: Gradus ad Parnassum

FUGUE SUBJECTS AND ANSWERS

Sing each fugue subject with letter names or fixed-do solfège, then follow it with its real answer (transpose the subject to the dominant key).

790. Bach: W.T.C., Book I, Fugue I

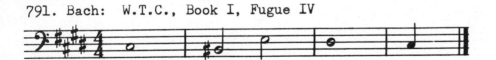

791. Bach: W.T.C., Book I, Fugue IV

792. Bach: W.T.C., Book I, Fugue VI

793. Bach: W.T.C., Book I, Fugue IX

Fugue subjects and answers.

794. Bach: W.T.C., Book I, Fugue XIV

795. Bach: W.T.C., Book II, Fugue XXIX

796. Bach: W.T.C., Book II, Fugue XXXII

797. Bach: W.T.C., Book II, Fugue XXXIII

798. Bach: W.T.C., Book II, Fugue XLII

799. Bach: W.T.C., Book II, Fugue XLVII

Supplementary materials.

CANON

     Sing the following canons, using letter names, solfège, or scale degree numbers.
     Transposition by clef will be helpful in these examples. Do not, however, alter the key signature of the <u>comes</u> (second voice).

800. Josquin: Missa Hercules dux Ferrariae, canon at the fifth

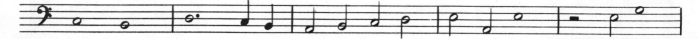

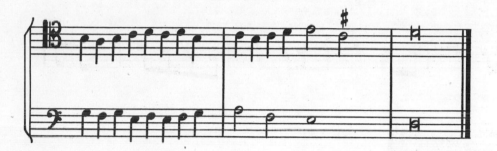

801. Bach: Goldberg Variations, Variation 6, canon at the second

802. Bach: Goldberg Variations, Variation 18, canon at the sixth

803. Bach: Perpetual canon for four voices

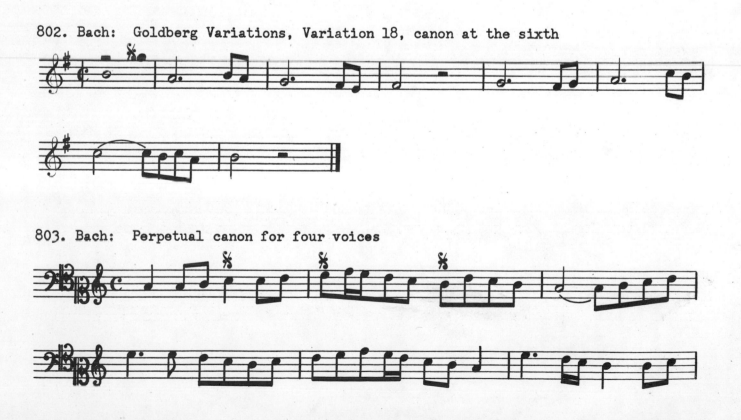

226

Supplementary materials.

Aspects of Voice Production

by Eldon Black

One very serious problem which arises in many sight-singing classes is the inability or reluctance of the sight-singer to produce sufficient volume. Often this deficiency results from nervousness, shyness, lack of confidence, fear of "sounding bad," and fear of singing wrong notes. It is obvious that the student cannot postpone the development of his sight-singing abilities until he can train his voice as an instrument and gain the confidence needed to eliminate the above mentioned causes of the problem. What can be done, then, to help alleviate the problems, and provide some possibility for remedy? The most effective solution lies in three areas: posture, breathing, and support.

Posture

For seated performance, the singer should sit well forward in his chair with his back erect and not touching the back of the chair. The chest should be comfortably high with shoulders relaxed, and both feet should be on the floor.

For standing performance, the singer should maintain erect posture with head and chest held high. The feet should be spread in comfortable stance with one foot slightly in front of the other. Once the chest has been lifted either in sitting or standing, that position should be sustained.

Breathing

With the chest in raised position, the singer should breathe deeply from the diaphragm, feeling expansion around the waist area, front, side, and back. The lungs should be completely filled and the raised chest should be maintained. Care should be taken that the chest not raise and lower with inhalation and exhalation.

Support

Once the singer has filled his lungs by lowering the diaphragm, the air must then be expelled from the lungs through the combined effort of the back, side, and stomach muscles. The following two exercises will enable the singer to get the proper feeling of the use of these muscles.

1. Take a full breath. Shout "Hey" very loudly. Do not let the chest drop. Feel the concentration in the muscles around the waist.
2. Take a full breath. Hiss as strongly as you can. This produces a

sustained tension of these muscles and creates the sensation the singer should experience while sustaining a tone or in singing a long legato phrase. Care should be taken again not to let the chest drop.

Posture, breathing, and support are but three significant aspects of good voice production, but they are of vital importance and should be worked on diligently.

Male members of sight-singing classes often have difficulty in singing the upper notes of exercises. In such cases, they should not hesitate to switch into their falsetto registers or transpose to a lower octave.

APPENDIX B

Chromatic Solfège

by Jerry Dean

Chromatic solfège is one of several possible systems for use in sight-singing. It is a "fixed-do" system; i.e., <u>do</u> is always pitch-class C. The basic solmisation syllables are used in conjunction with chromatic variants for alterations of the basic syllables. Chromatic solfège is a monosyllabic replacement for letter names, which are awkward due to the fact that chromatic alterations have two or more syllables (F-sharp, B-double flat, etc.).

The following chart gives the syllables used in chromatic solfège. Each vertical column contains two or three enharmonic versions of a pitch-class. The vowels are pronounced as in Latin.[1] The added consonant "s" means "one half step sharper" and the added "f" means "one half step flatter."

	PC: 0	1	2	3	4	5	6	7	8	9	10	11	0
Double sharps:		dis		ris			fis		sis		lis		
Sharps:		di		ri	mis		fi		si		li	tis	
Basic:	do		re		mi	fa		so		la		ti	do
Flats:		ra		me	fe		se		le		te	de	
Double flats:	raf		mef	fef		sef		lef		tef	def		

---
[1] The "e" is usually given the long "a" sound, but a short "e" pronunciation (as in "neck") eliminates the troublesome diphthong.

Indexes

All references are to example numbers.

COMPOSER

Wagner 625, 626
Webern 660, 661, 662, 663, 664
Wellesz 653
White, Matthew 550

CLEF

Example numbers in parentheses refer to exercises involving more than one clef.

Alto clef 428, 429, 430, 431, 432, 433, 434, 435, 436, 437, 438, 439, (462), (463), 494, 495, 496, 503, 506, 512, 516, 518, 521, 523, (524), 532, 538, (539), 548, 552, 564, 579, 592, 598, 601, 607, 616, 635, 638, 658, (660), 667, 672, 678, 721, 722, 726, 729, 740, 741, 752, 753, 761, 762, 763, 778, 780, 782, 785, 786, 787, 788, 789

Baritone clef 458, 459, 460, (461)

Bass clef 268, 270, 271, 275, 277, 280, 284, 285, 287, 290, 291, 293, 296, 297, 300, 304, 306, 309, 310, 313, 316, 317, 320, 323, 326, 327, 330, 336, 337, 338, 341, 342, 343, 344, 355, 356, 357, 358, 360, 361, 363, 367, 370, 374, 375, 378, 379, 381, 383, 384, 385, 387, 390, 391, 393, 396, 399, 402, 403, 405, 407, 408, 410, 411, 412, 415, 416, 418, 419, 424, 427, (463), 497, 500, 501, (508), (509), 511, (524), 525, 535, 537, 540, 559, 563, 566, (567), 573, 574, 577, 578, 591, 600, (606), (608), 615, 624, 625, 626, 628, 630, 634, 639, 642, 644, 652, 653, (659), 668, (669), 671, 673, 674, 675, 676, 680, 685, (686), 695, 697, 698, 699, 701, 703, 704, 707, 709, 711, (714), 718, 719, 720, 725, 728, 730, 733, 749, 750, 751, 774, 777, 781, 791, 794, 795, 797, 799, (800), (803)

Mezzo-soprano clef 456, 457, (803)

Soprano clef 452, 453, 454, 455, (463)

Tenor clef 440, 441, 442, 443, 444, 445, 446, 447, 448, 449, 450, 451, (461), (462), (463), (469), 498, 499, 504, 505, (509), 513, 515, 519, 528, 529, (530), 531, 533, 534, 565, 595, (608), 612, (659), 677, 724, 732, 758, 759, 760, 783, 784, (800), (803)

TEXTURE

Two voices 8, 14, 20, 32, 38, 44, 56, 62, 68, 80, 86, 95, 100, 109, 114, 121, 127, 136, 141, 149, 154, 164, 169, 179, 184, 194, 199, 223, 233, 263, 264, 265, 462, 468, 469, 503, 515, 522, 524, 527, 539, 545, 570, 583, 612, 685, 686, 689, 714, 782, 783, 784, 785, 786, 787, 788, 789, 800, 801, 802

Three voices 509, 510, 530, 550, 606, 669

Four voices 463, 508, 567, 803